RUNNING FOR THEIR LIVES

"One man's incredible story of overcoming
adversity to save the lives of at-risk youth"

FREDERICK DRYDEN

"One man's incredible story of overcoming adversity to save the lives of at-risk youth."

RUNNING FOR THEIR LIVES: FREDERICK DRYDEN'S STORY
As told to Nikki Rottenberg

This is a true story; however, some names have been changed to protect the identity of certain people.

To contact Liberty For Youth or to make a donation:
905-297-7929 • www.libertyforyouth.org
1925 King Street East, Hamilton, ON L8K 1V9

Unless otherwise noted, Scripture quotations are taken from The New International Version Copyright © 1986 by Holman Bible Publishers

Printed in Canada
ISBN 978-0-9809171-5-4 (paperback)

COVER DESIGN
Oeun Long

COMPLETE BOOK DESIGN, TYPESETTING AND PRINTING
John VanDuzer, WISHART.NET

BACK COVER PHOTO
Rudy Tijerino

TABLE OF CONTENTS

Photo: Christopher Andrade

FOREWORD

IT IS INDEED MY pleasure to introduce Frederick Dryden's book "Running For Their Lives." I have known Frederick for many years and immediately was inspired with his vision for Liberty For Youth and dream of leading vulnerable youth down the right life path to success.

Frederick is a proud husband and a wonderful parent to his children. He is steadfast and loyal to his family who support the sacrifice necessary to successfully accomplish his many goals and his vision for Liberty For Youth. His passion, commitment, selflessness and loyalty to the youth that he serves is relentless. He has provided mentoring, leadership and coaching to his amazing staff, while being conscious of a succession plan, stability, and sustainability for Liberty For Youth.

It is time for Frederick to tell his story to the world, and this is why I proudly endorse his wonderful book. Reading it, I promise you will be truly inspired! ENJOY!

Ron Foxcroft
CEO and Founder Fox 40 International Inc,
and CEO Fluke Transport Ltd.

PREFACE

ALMOST IMMEDIATELY AFTER I said "Yes, Frederick, I would be happy to drive the support van for your run," I began to have second thoughts. Did I really want to spend three weeks slowly driving a van from Ottawa to Hamilton behind this passionate, energetic man? What was to gain? How was this run going to help youth who were connected to the Liberty For Youth programs? What would I do if Frederick was injured along the journey? Was this man really considering doing this? Was he thinking clearly? Was I?

Run 650 kilometres in 21 days to raise $650,000 to sustain vital programming for at-risk youth. That was the mission. That was Frederick's mission and he needed my help.

All my second thoughts and questions are distant memories as I reflect back on the amazing accomplishment Frederick achieved for the youth at risk. Frederick's three-week marathon trek accomplished more than I ever thought possible. As you read this book, you will begin to understand how important this run was to help the youth in Liberty For Youth programs.

Frederick begins this book telling the story of how he was an at-risk youth. You will begin to understand why the following three E's: Engagement, Encouragement and Empowerment were so critical in helping him turn his life around. He shares how they were the keys to his own redemption and the vision driving Liberty For Youth today.

As you read this book, you will begin to appreciate how Frederick's *Run for Youth* symbolizes Frederick's run through life: his passion, his energy, his hopeful enthusiasm, and his willingness to do whatever it takes to reach those who need it most.

As you read this book, I believe you too will be engaged, encouraged and empowered to take on life's challenges with renewed hope and determination.

George Van Kampen

DEDICATION

TO MY LOVING WIFE, Tanya, and children, Chanice, Justus, Jason, and Julius. You have sacrificed so much, sometimes without even knowing what you were giving up. I thank you and will always love you.

To youth everywhere, never let your past mistakes define you; rather, let them refine you.

Love, Frederick

CHAPTER 1

BECOMING AT-RISK

BEFORE I WAS BORN, my parents separated. My father decided to move to Canada in hopes of providing a better life for his children. My mother remained in Jamaica with her seven children: Norman, Lorna, Errol, David, Paris, Carol and Barbara. Shortly after my father left, my mother discovered she was expecting me.

My mother struggled financially. The work she did was laborious and didn't pay much. Caring for her seven kids already stretched her resources and energy. Bringing another child home meant she'd need to find a second job to make ends meet, but she knew with God's help somehow she'd manage.

I was born in October of 1971. My early years growing up in Montego Bay, Jamaica were stable and carefree. Our family was poor, but we had each other, and that made all the difference (pictured at left).

We lived off nature; plucking fruits and berries that grew wild. And because there was limited transportation, my siblings and I walked to and from school. Some days the trek was long and unexciting. Sometimes we played and entertained each other along the way. One time we were even chased by a cow.

WHEN MY MOM CAME home from work in the evenings, she often collapsed on the porch exhausted. I wanted to comfort her in any way I could. I'd make her a cup of tea and then fan her while she fell asleep. The bond between us was strong.

Sometimes, in between her jobs, my mother brought us lunch at school. I still remember the taste of those Jamaican patties. They were spicy and delicious. Looking back, I often wonder where she found the time to bring us lunch.

When she cooked meals, my mother would always make a couple of extra plates and place them on the counter. She admonished us to not touch them. My brothers and I, especially, still hungry after we finished our meals, wanted to eat the 'extra' food, but she'd shake her head and say "No, those are just-in-case plates." Our mother kept the food for unexpected company, even if it was a stranger who was lost, homeless or in need. She always wanted to ensure she had something to offer them. The following day, if no one had come by, we could eat the 'extra food.'

Not only was my mother generous, she was also a savvy negotiator with market vendors and creditors. I remember when I was seven years old, I would wake up early in the mornings to go to the market with my mother. Before we left home, she'd put $50 in my left back pocket, $20 in my right back pocket, $10 bills in my front left pocket and $5 bills in my right front pocket. She went over and over with me, which pocket held what and instructed me to remember. When negotiating with market vendors I had to recall exactly which pocket each bill was in. If I made a mistake and pulled out a larger bill, the marketer would see the extra money and charge us more. My mother also imparted to me an entrepreneurial spirit when she taught me how to sell eggs and ice in the neighbourhood. She wanted to prepare me with skills I would later need in life.

When my father established himself in Canada, he offered his children the option to come and live with him. He promised that we would enjoy a better life, get a good education and have more opportunities than we would in Jamaica. My mother reluctantly agreed.

By 1982, my siblings Paris and Carol were already with our father in Canada. I, being the youngest, was the last to join them.

The day my mother took me to the Montego Bay airport, the temperature was a stifling 40 degrees Celsius. I had never been on a plane before and I was leaving behind my mother, my five oldest siblings and my carefree life in Jamaica.

I stared at the huge planes on the tarmac. A voice over a loudspeaker instructed those flying to Toronto to proceed to the gate. I hugged my mother tightly before I boarded the plane. During the flight, I was full of emotions. I was very close to my mom and didn't want to leave her, but I was curious to finally meet my father. Excitement welled up within me to reunite with my brother and sister. They had told me many stories about life in Canada. I looked forward to watching cartoons, eating cereal and seeing snow. Finally, as the plane began the descent into Toronto, I stared out the window, fascinated by the tall buildings and bright lights.

MY FATHER AND siblings were waiting for me when I arrived at Pearson Airport. Having never met him prior, I worried that my father wouldn't accept me. But that wasn't the case at all. He happily welcomed me.

When we stepped outside to go to the car, I shivered in the cold air. As we drove past Georgian Bay, the temperature dropped to -40 degrees, the exact opposite of what it was when I left Montego Bay. These two weather extremes proved to be symbolic of the drastic changes that would soon occur in my life.

The drive to my new home in Collingwood was exciting. I had never seen snow before. Seeing the little white flakes fascinated me. Once settled in, my brother introduced me to break dancing and the TV station Much Music. I listened to songs by Michael Jackson, Tina Turner and Twisted Sister. I watched the movie *Ghostbusters* and ate potato chips. I especially loved to watch cartoons. In Jamaica, we had only one or two channels that came on for only a few hours a day. My first few weeks in Canada were full of new and wonderful experiences. Things, however, would soon start to change and break down.

When my father registered me for school he decided to change my name to Clint. At school, when the teacher asked me to stand up and introduce myself, I stuttered and stammered. I got mixed up and started to say Freder... but then quickly changed it to Clint. They laughed and mocked me, "Dummy, doesn't even know his own name." I felt so ashamed. It was also the first time in my life I experienced racism. There were only three African-Canadian families living in the area. I was mocked for my strong Jamaican accent, endured vulgar comments about my skin colour, and was teased about having an afro. I was constantly trying to fit in. One time during the winter, a few boys told me to lick the fence. They made it sound like fun, like something everyone did. I leaned over and stuck my tongue on the metal. To my horror, I realized they had tricked me. I couldn't get my tongue unstuck. The boys roared with laughter and left me there. Even though this mirrors a scene from the classic movie *A Christmas Story*, there was nothing funny about it. I felt humiliated. I was also in pain. A teacher eventually came and helped me, but the damage was done. I realized I couldn't trust these 'new friends.' Back home in Jamaica, everyone had each other's back. Not here. I decided that I would stop trying to fit in and try to become invisible.

DOWNWARD SPIRAL

DESPITE MY EFFORTS, I didn't become invisible. The teasing and intense bullying continued. My sister Carol and I would leave school as fast as we could to escape the boys that would try to beat us up every day. Still, it got worse. One afternoon Carol came home crying hysterically. We had a very strong bond and yet she couldn't find the words to tell me what was wrong. Soon after, a social worker visited our house. Then suddenly, our father sent her back to Jamaica. She returned a few months later. Although I knew something bad had happened to her, no one explained anything to me. She later shared that she had been a victim of sexual abuse. As her brother, I felt responsible for what happened to her. I was angry with myself for not being able to protect her. I never knew that I too, would soon become a victim like she had been.

My family eventually moved away from Collingwood.

My father found a place in Toronto and we settled there. He began a new relationship, rented an apartment and brought his partner and her children to live with us. My father was a truck driver and did whatever he thought best to provide for us. He was often gone for weeks, sometimes months at a time. While he was away, his new partner looked after us. She was not a kind woman. There was never enough food in the house for my siblings and me to eat. We were always starving. However, her children ate well. Somehow they were able to 'find' the food, while we went without.

I often thought about my mom; she would never stand for this. I wrote her a letter and told her about the awful hardships we were going through. Somehow, before I could send it, my father's partner found and read the letter. She became enraged and punished me by locking me in the basement. She forced me to rewrite the letter to my mom telling her how great it was in Canada. I was so isolated, so scared and so hopeless.

WHEN I TURNED THIRTEEN, I was sexually abused. One of the older teens in the house came into my room at night. She sexually abused me. I lay there numb, in complete silence. I was so confused. She was supposed to be like a stepsister to me. I was so scared and ashamed as other members of the household lay sleeping in the bottom bunk below.

I never told anyone. I was afraid that if I resisted I would get beat up. I was afraid that I would get laughed at if I complained. As I lay there with tears rolling down my face, I was afraid, thinking that there was no one to turn to.

This sexual abuse continued for several months. It left me confused in many ways and my self-esteem plummeted even more.

My young life had been shattered. I became an at-risk youth. I found myself without any friends. I couldn't trust anyone anymore. I went days without eating because often there was never enough food in the house. At times, I was locked in the dingy basement and the water was shut off so I couldn't take a shower. Other times, I had to use a hose attached to the washing machine.

To make matters worse, cockroaches were everywhere. They even crawled on me. I remember how I used to cover my face to prevent them from getting into my eyes, mouth and nose. One day though, I started having bad headaches and a burning in my ear. At school, they referred me to a doctor who told me this discomfort was due to insects having laid eggs inside my ears. I don't know why, but I felt ashamed – like it was my fault. Somehow it communicated to me that I was disgusting and worthless, like a rat on the street.

My home life had become too unbearable. When my dad's partner held a knife to my throat, I finally left home. I was just 15. I stayed at friends' places, but not for long. I moved constantly. Three or four times I returned 'home' only to find the same old chaos as before. I'd take off again, find a factory job, earn a bit of cash and rent a cheap basement apartment. From the erratic way I lived, and the constant nervous tension, I developed stomach issues. Whenever I showed up at my friends' homes, I went on an eating binge. I would wolf down whatever food I could get my hands on to fill my stomach, as it could be days before I would eat again. As a result of this eating pattern, my stomach issues became worse. Not understanding my situation, some of my friends' mothers told me not to come back to their homes.

In spite of everything, I remembered my mother's work ethic and how she laboured at two jobs to support my siblings and me. Her resolve to do what she needed to do had made an impact on me. No matter how chaotic my life got, I worked to pay my rent and stayed in school.

CHAPTER 2

THE LIBERTY TO CHOOSE

DURING MY HIGH SCHOOL years, I was burnt out. I found it difficult to focus on my school work. My accent was still strong and even though my native language was English, I was put in an ESL class that was referred to as a booster program. This particular class was filled with kids from underprivileged families and kids who had immigrated from non-English speaking countries. The other students laughed at us 'booster kids' and called us stupid.

Again, I was identified as a 'dummy.' Sometimes to avoid the ridicule, I hid in the hallway until class started. I'd then have to get a late slip. I would often skip class altogether.

One particular day, I received the results of a math test I had taken. I stared at my failed mark and decided I was done with school. I got up and walked out of the class. When I heard footsteps behind me, I turned around and saw my teacher, Mr. Dodd. The man inspired me to stay in the class. "I believe in you," he said. "Last week you scored an eighty-five on an independent study test. You can still pass the class and if you come to see me for tutoring on Tuesdays and Thursdays, I'll even bring breakfast." My eyes lit up. I didn't care too much for the tutoring, but the mention of food motivated me. After a couple of months, I passed the class with a seventy-five percent average. To this day, I still hear Mr. Dodd's 'footsteps' and feel the tremendous difference his engagement made in my life.

With this passing grade, I could now play on the school basketball team. As a player, I was part of something bigger than myself. I was part of a team which was, in a way, a type of family. I was accountable to my coach and teammates. Whenever I heard my name mentioned on the school announcements for the most points scored or MVP, I felt proud. My positive experience with the teacher and the team built up my confidence in the school system.

However, I still faced challenges. Being on my own at such a young age seemed to attract negative influences. People came into my life and showered me with attention for their own ulterior motives. I will never forget the guy with the Rolls Royce; although, I do forget where and how I met him. I was sixteen at the time and he had money. Lots of it. I knew something was fishy, but I liked the feeling of having someone looking out for me.

Eventually, the predictable day came. He picked me up and drove to a plaza. We parked and he proposed an idea. He described how I could help him rob a local business. The suggestion took me by surprise. I didn't want to lose the friendship, but I also didn't want to commit a robbery. After going through the possible scenarios and disastrous out-comes in mind, I said no. I wouldn't do it. He became angry and kicked me out of the car. I never saw him again.

Again, when I turned seventeen, I began hanging around with older guys on the streets. They befriended us 'lost boys' and made us feel like we belonged. They took us to places like McDonald's and bought us whatever we wanted. They brought us to football games across the Canadian-American border. I thought they were safe because they never asked us to do anything bad. They said they liked spoiling us because they remembered how hard it was on the streets. How naïve I was. On one occasion, we were in the United States as we had been several times before. We were walking around a mall together when the police approached us. I thought to myself, it must be a case of mistaken identity. I hadn't done anything wrong and had never been in trouble with the law before. The police began questioning the older guys and seemed to recognize them. The younger guys and I stood there frozen, unable to comprehend what was happening. The police began reading all of us our rights and put handcuffs on my wrists. My body started shaking and I went numb. We were brought down to the police station where we were informed that our backpacks were stuffed with drugs and stolen goods.

They used us. I was terrified. I soon learned that the older guys had been well known to the police and it wasn't the first time they had done this to younger, unsuspecting victims. At that moment, I hated everything about my life. Thankfully, my friends and I were not charged. Upon our release, one officer called me back. He sat me down and shared his own troubled life story. He looked at me, straight in the eye and said, "Use everything you went through, all the bad stuff, as a weapon to create change for your future."

The words penetrated my heart. The officer bought me a ticket and put me on a bus back to Toronto. During the long drive home, I thought about what the cop had said. "It's not what you did, but it's about what you'll do. It's about your future." That ten-minute talk from the officer was a defining moment in my life. Like an arrow hitting its mark, that brief encounter changed me. A year later at my high school graduation ceremony, tears filled my eyes as I reflected on the officer's words and for the first time felt hope for my future.

MY SUNFLOWER

SOON AFTER HIGH SCHOOL, my girlfriend became pregnant. I became a father to a beautiful little girl. When I looked at her, I kept thinking to myself, *Oh my gosh, I'm a father! I'm really a father. Someone is now depending on me. I have to live. I have to provide.* From the first moment I laid my eyes on her, I knew I would do everything in my power to give her a better life. I adored everything about her. She became my little sunflower. She was the motivation I needed to clean up my life. It was my little girl who drew me away from the all the negative influences and inspired me to really plan a better future (pictured at right).

I got a job at a local hospital as a porter. When my daughter was old enough, I started taking her every other weekend. At the time, I lived in a small basement apartment. We would curl up together, munch on snacks, watch cartoons, and laugh over the silly, animated characters. I still remember watching Disney's *The Jungle Book*. My daughter made a comment in her sweet little voice about the buzzing bees, "You gonna burn out." Hearing her say the simplicity of those words just hit me. My little girl was teaching me to stop rushing around. She taught me to appreciate life. I was working hard but I needed a strategy to improve our lives.

I worked from five in the morning until three in the afternoon. Some days, I picked up my daughter after school and
spent time with her. In the evenings, I returned to the hospital
to work another shift. I worked hard and saved my money. I
told my supervisor I'd work as many shifts as she would give
me. I was determined to build a career at the hospital.

I was known for my dedication and unwavering
commitment. In January 1999, Toronto was hit with a major

snowstorm. Many staff called in to say they were unable to come to work. I, however, trudged on foot through the extreme blizzard down numerous blocks to the hospital. I worked not only my own shift, but filled in for some of the other staff as well. The weather had become so awful that I stayed at the hospital for a few days to help out.

Coworkers would tell me I was over-committed. But they never experienced what I did. I remembered the terrible poverty back in Jamaica. To this day, I vividly remember my mother's face as creditors repossessed furniture she was just a few payments away from owning. We just stood there as they emptied the room. It tore my heart knowing how hard my mother worked to make those payments and hearing her soft tears later that night.

The experience affected me so much so, that even to this day, I hate using credit. It helped shape my view on finances. I sought out ways I could become financially independent. I devoured books on finances and self-development. My favourites were *The Wealthy Barber*, by David Chilton and *Maximize the Moment*, by T.D. Jakes. The books set out practical steps.

I started making financial changes. Two years earlier, I had purchased my first car, an Acura Integra. It was my pride and joy. After the car was paid off, I decided to sell it. When it sold, I got half the value I paid for it. It stunned me that I had worked so hard to pay off the car and got so little back in return. It had been such a waste of money. The money I made from the sale of the car, I invested at the bank. Instead of driving, I bussed everywhere and saved the additional money I would have spent on gas, insurance, and maintenance.

To cut back further, I moved into a rooming house. I shared a bathroom with six other people, but it didn't bother me. I saw the move as sharing expenses to save money. Determined to achieve my goal of financial independence, I was resolute to do whatever it took. I spent little and saved much.

When I was in my twenties, I put a $25,000 down payment on a semi-detached home in Brampton. The following year, I would have to pay another $20,000 for the remaining down payment. This time I knew, unlike the car that decreased in value when sold, the value of a home would increase. While the house was being built, I often went and sat inside the frame. Being there kept me motivated and reminded me of what I was working towards.

AIMING HIGHER

DURING THIS TIME, I realized my career options were limited at the hospital. I decided to obtain my licence to sell RESP's. There wasn't a guarantee I would be successful and I still needed financial stability for my daughter and me. So, I made the tough decision to rent out the new home instead of living there. The rental income would provide enough margin to launch my new career. This proved to be a great move. My commission in the first weekend equalled what I would have made in two weeks at my current job. This was definitely more lucrative and exciting as I operated with that entrepreneurial spirit instilled in me by my mother. Within a year I resigned from my position at the hospital and worked full time selling RESP's. I bought a second home. This success gave me confidence and I finally felt stable. The love of my daughter and my work brought me joy. Yet, I was still missing something.

BRINGING MOM TO CANADA

I WAS IN MY early twenties when my older brother and I decided to bring our mom to live in Canada. At 65-years-old she had retired from working and we were concerned about her health. We initially invited her to visit Canada to see if she would like it.

After her arrival (pictured below), I arranged to have dinner with my mother and father. I had never seen my parents sit down at a table and eat together. During the dinner, I didn't eat. I had hungered for that sense of family for so long that I just needed to watch my parents share a meal together. It was a surreal experience. My mind wandered to having a family of my own. Would I one day sit down at a table with a wife and children? In a home where we all lived together, ate together, and dreamed together? Little did I know how full my table would one day be.

CHAPTER 3

THE POWER OF A CHANGED LIFE

BEING AN RESP CONSULTANT came with many benefits. I created my own schedule, worked all over the city, and constantly interacted with new people. My business relied on referrals. So, when a client invited me to attend her place of worship, I agreed without hesitation. I would definitely get my five referrals there. I settled into a seat near the back. The Pastor encouraged everyone to say hello to the person next to them. I reached over to shake hands with a potential client and then I spotted the most beautiful woman. I passed the person next to me and walked a few seats over. I shook her hand and told her it was nice to meet her. She responded with a raised eyebrow and a slight smile. I went back to my seat and tried not to stare at her for the next hour. I forgot about getting referrals. I just wanted her number. After the service, I approached her again and introduced myself. She was cautiously smiling and told me her name was Tanya. I asked for her phone number and she politely turned me down. "Sorry,

I don't give my number out." Her response didn't deter me. I continued to talk to her and discovered she was attending Mohawk College. She loved studying business, but none of her friends did. When I heard that, my eyes lit up. "That's my field of expertise. Let me help you study sometime," I blurted out. Then her eyes lit up. I left with her email address. A few weeks later, I drove from Toronto to meet her at the college library. Our connection was so strong. I learned she was community-minded and passionate about helping the needy. She volunteered at multiple organizations, loved children, and possessed an exuberant faith. I constantly searched for ways to spend time with this inspiring woman. Tanya invited me to her church in downtown Hamilton. Sunday morning came and I headed onto the QEW to see her. In no way did I foresee how that day would change the course of so many people's lives. I sat in the pew listening to the pastor's sermon. "Who is willing to go feed the hungry? Who is willing to care for the infirmed? Who is willing to visit those in prison?" he resounded. These words pierced my heart. I shifted in my seat. He continued, "Who will help the broken, the lost, the drug addict? Who is willing to go?"

The words, like liquid fire, burned inside me. That week, the words played over and over again in my mind, 'visit those in prison' I considered my own troubled background and wondered if somehow I could use what I had lived and overcome to help someone else. I had been one of the lost, one of the broken, a street kid, running wild, and living on life's edge. I knew the lifestyle all too well and what it felt like to live with no hope. I was convicted and compelled to do something.

There was a youth detention centre very close to the church where the words had stirred my heart. So, I would start there. With exhilaration and apprehension, I contacted the Barton Street Jail.

Living Rock Founder, Al Craig, was the facility's chaplain at the time. He graciously met with me. As I sat in Pastor Craig's office, I glanced at all the books that lined the shelves. In desperation I blurted out, "Can I borrow some of these? I want to help, but I don't know how or what to do." Pastor Craig smiled. "Frederick, I can give you all these books, but what you need is the heart to make a difference in the lives of these youth." I thought for a moment and assured him, "I do. I really do. But where do I start?"

With an affirming nod, Pastor Craig responded, "Good. The first thing is to enrol in our safety training program. It will prepare you to work inside the prison." "I'm in," I said, without hesitation.

IT ALL STARTS WITH 'ONE'

AFTER COMPLETING THE SAFETY training program, I was paired up with a volunteer who led group Bible studies, named Jane. She instructed me not to speak, but to only observe how the meeting was facilitated.

I sat next to Jane as I watched the youth file into the small room and take their seats. Some glanced over at me. I smiled, feeling both nervous and excited to be there. I listened intently as Jane shared passages from the Bible. Fifteen minutes after the start of the group, one of the boys pointed at me and asked, "What's he doing here?"

I waved my hand to signal that I wasn't supposed to talk. Jane continued teaching. A few minutes later, the same boy asked about me again. Nothing was said, but when the boy asked a third time, Jane leaned over to me and asked if I would like to say something.

"But you told me not to speak," I whispered back.

"I'm telling you now, if you like, you can say a few words."

I looked around the room at the young faces staring at me, waiting for me to say something. My heart thumped as I thought of something to say at a moment's notice. I decided to share some of my own troubled past. I spoke about being lost, broken, and angry. I told them how terrified I was in grade nine when my best friend Vince was shot six times.

I explained my perilous first date. She had a fancy car and invited me in. I climbed into the passenger side thinking I hit the first date jackpot. When police stopped us, a few blocks away, I realized the car had been stolen and my excitement turned to fear. The girl stepped on the gas and outran the cops. She screeched to a halt, we jumped out of the car and took off running. As I ran, I was afraid of getting shot in the back. That was life on the edge. Although I was not a bad kid, I got into many bad situations. The youth hung onto my every word. My life reflected their lives.

Afterwards, Jane handed me a note. It read: *You are ready to start your own program. God has given you the gift of wisdom through teaching youth.*

When I read those words, fear gripped me. *I'm ready to start my own program? How could she say that?* I needed Jane's guidance. I needed someone to show me the way to reach those young people.

Three weeks passed. I stayed away from the jail. I was too scared to go back, but the conviction in my heart to help young people was so strong that by the fourth week, I couldn't stay away anymore. I returned to the jail and asked to see the youth who had interrupted the Bible study by demanding that I speak. To my surprise, 15-year-old Clay was glad to see me. We sat and talked for an hour. When I got up to leave, I promised Clay that I would come back every week and meet with him until his release.

At the time, I was living in Toronto but kept my promise to Clay. Every Wednesday I drove to the Barton Street Jail in Hamilton to visit him. Six months later he was transferred to an open custody facility in Kitchener. The drive to Kitchener was more difficult for me as it was a longer distance, but I continued my weekly visits to Clay as promised, encouraging and mentoring him. Connecting with him stirred my heart and my past. There were so many teens marginalized and at-risk like I was. I wanted to do more to help but wasn't sure how.

It was during this time that my relationship with Tanya was deepening and I knew she was the one I wanted to spend the rest of my life with. I moved to Hamilton and bought a perfect little home for Tanya and my daughter. It was time to propose. We met at the picturesque Dundurn Castle for this unforgettable moment. I popped the question. She said yes. Second greatest moment of my life. As I was soaking it all in, Tanya interrupted, "I love you, and you have been through so much. You have to make peace with the past and deal with the unforgiveness you are carrying." She hesitated and then continued, "Before I'll marry you, you need to forgive the people who hurt you."

Her words stunned me. "Does that mean you won't marry me?" I asked. "If you're not willing to forgive and let go of your past, you're not letting me marry you," she responded.

Feeling rejected, I left shaking my head. As I drove home, Tanya's words played over in my mind. *If you're not willing to forgive, you won't let me marry you.* Life had turned around. I was fine. I moved on. Why did this matter? Deep inside, of course, I knew she was right. My difficult past crippled me now and then with nightmares, negative memories, and even anxiety. Inside I was still hurting, broken and angry. It was time to take action. I called Tanya and asked if she'd help me write a letter to the people who had hurt me. Tanya wholeheartedly agreed. I found it extremely hard writing the letter. I cried as the painful memories surfaced. It dawned on me, how much my past was holding me hostage. I wrote the letter and chose to forgive the people who had hurt me and my family. Afterward, I turned and looked at this woman I had come to love. With her strong faith and convictions, Tanya was helping me heal.

When the letter was written, I called my father and asked if he would come with me to deliver it in person. The drive there felt like an eternity. I was about to confront my pain and past, something I had been running away from for a long time.

When we pulled up to their home I froze, not wanting to go inside. My father encouraged me to continue. We knocked and they invited us in. At first, my abusers denied doing anything wrong, but after a while, they began opening up about their personal struggles. They shared about the mental illness they had experienced and abuse they suffered. Learning of their painful struggles made it easier for me to let go of the bitterness and resentments I had held against them. My father was shocked. He had been unaware of the level of abuse that I had experienced during his time away at work.

When I left their home that day, I felt as if five hundred pounds had been lifted off me. I now understood that sometimes it's important to go backwards in order to move forward. I am thankful Tanya pushed me to move out of my pain to be free and to live a richer life. Now, we could plan a wedding.

CHAPTER 4

THE INCEPTION OF LIBERTY FOR YOUTH

I HAD VISITED CLAY at the youth detention centre for the past year. When the 16-year-old was released, his mother and stepfather had a request for me. They asked if I would consider becoming Clay's legal guardian. They worried if he stayed with them, he'd slip back into his old ways. The gang had already come around and tried to lure Clay back. The pull to hang out with his old friends was strong. His mom told me they had seen drastic changes in their son's life since my involvement.

Stunned at their request, I didn't know what to say. I loved Clay, and I knew how much he had changed, but I was engaged to be married. Tanya would move in after the wedding which was only three months away. A million thoughts ran through my mind. As much as I wanted to say yes, I needed to step back. Tanya was my priority. She was so excited to start our life together. I couldn't throw anything like this on her. Or could I?

The following day, I called Tanya. We chatted excitedly about plans for our wedding. However, my mind drifted off as I thought about Clay and the request his mother and step-father had made. I shook my head. I wanted desperately to help Clay, but I also wanted to make Tanya happy and keep her safe. Even over the phone, she could tell I wasn't myself. She tenderly spoke, "Are you ok? What's wrong?"

I hesitated for a moment before revealing Clay's parents' request for me to become a guardian of their son. Without hesitation, Tanya asked, "Why wouldn't you?" I answered, "You don't understand what this means. Let's discuss this in person." Immediately I went and picked her up. We got a cup of tea and stayed in the parking lot. I restarted the discussion. "Clay would be moving in with us. He had serious charges. Not minor ones." I continued, "He has made progress; he has potential, but you need to understand." She stopped me, "Who am I to say no? We need to live to help others. We can do this." My eyes widened. I stared at her, speechless. At that moment I knew beyond a shadow of a doubt, this kind-hearted woman was my soul mate and that there was a 'calling' on my life to serve youth.

After I dropped Tanya off at work, I rushed back home and called Clay's parents. I could hardly contain my excite-ment as I told them that Tanya and I would become legal guardians of their son. They couldn't hide their gratitude. I wasted no time preparing to bring Clay home. I laughed to myself, thinking about Tanya and I becoming parents to an over six-foot tall teenager.

The following months flew by. I completed the necessary legal paperwork to register Clay for school and probation. I used my own resources to renovate the basement of the house to accommodate Clay. I instructed the contractors to make three bedrooms, a kitchen, a bathroom, a recreational room and a separate entrance. Although it was just Clay moving in, I felt in my heart, there would be more boys to follow. I wanted to ensure the youth would have everything they needed. Once the renovations were complete, Clay moved in, excited to start his new lease at life. Tanya and I were married three months later (pictured below) with Clay as one of my groomsmen.

EVERYTHING I DID LED me in a direction to influence and transform youth. We started mentoring more teens. Clay's friends from school made up the majority of the initial group.

He told his friend, Danny, who was in trouble with the law, about what we had done for him. When Danny ended up in a detention centre, he reached out to us and asked if we would help him like we had helped Clay. Danny asked if I would act as a 'surety' and take full responsibility for him. In order to do that, I would have to put my home up as an asset, attend all court meetings and ensure all conditions of his bail order were obeyed.

I knew of Danny. We had met him a few times when Clay brought him to our home. I knew that Danny's mother was a drug addict and that he had never met his incarcerated father. He was a good kid in bad circumstances. We agreed to help Danny if he attended school and participated in our mentorship group. Danny agreed to follow those rules. He moved into the basement apartment with Clay and became another one of our 'sons.' Soon another boy contacted us. He was out on probation, had no family in Canada, and needed a place to stay. We couldn't turn him away.

Three at-risk teens now lived in our home. Although the boys generally got along well, issues arose from time to time. Once, I was in a meeting when I received a call from Tanya. Two of the boys had gotten into a fight and one had gone through a wall. I still wonder how Tanya separated them. Both boys were over six feet tall.

Moving forward, I would separate the youth at times and have them take turns accompanying me, if possible, to prevent any potential disagreements in my absence. But I knew that I needed more hands on deck. I began recruiting mentors to assist me with the youth who lived in my home. Together we developed and incorporated lessons on the importance of reconciliation and offered incentives for non-violent behaviour.

Most of the danger we experienced was not from the youth themselves but from negative past associations. We stood strong when gang members came and loomed outside our house. They had tracked Clay down and tried to entice him back into the gang. Their presence was intimidating, but Clay diplomatically declined and eventually they left.

A month later, Tanya and I heard loud voices coming from the basement. I rushed downstairs and instantly felt the heavy tension in the room. Five gang members had returned to the house and this time they would not take no for an answer. I spoke to the boys carefully choosing my words and trying to discern the situation. To lighten the mood, I offered them some pizza, but it was evident they were not comfortable with me being there. They finally said to each other, "Let's go out for a walk," and forced Clay to leave the house. It would be hours before he returned.

Tanya and I realized the gang members were not going away easily and the situation wouldn't be a quick fix. I knew there was only so much we could do for Clay. Ultimately Clay had to decide how he wanted to proceed with his life. It was during this time that Tanya and I came up with the motto *Giving youth the Liberty to choose.* We were so proud that Clay chose to come back home. The gang never bothered him again.

We had to be hopeful and yet remain careful at all times. One night, Tanya came home alone and was startled by a youth who suddenly emerged from the dark, his hands all bloody. He had been in a fight and hid behind a tree, waiting for us to arrive. He wanted our help. Tanya recognized him; his name was Marcel. He had been involved in programming for several months. He was a victim of Fetal Alcohol Syndrome and we had great compassion for him. He was often a target for bullies; something I knew all too well. I was at a nearby grocery store when Tanya called me. I rushed home to bring the youth to the hospital. Thankfully, he was okay and continued to attend our program.

Every youth was unique. Yet every need required the same thing – *time.* We couldn't just shut them out during moments of crisis even if it was outside of programming hours. Night times were especially crazy. Sometimes the boys couldn't sleep. I remembered experiencing that myself. Nightmares or flashbacks troubled them and they wanted to talk into the early morning hours. Tanya and I were newlyweds and it was hard finding time for ourselves. We had also decided that we wanted to start a family. In 2005, our first son was born and within four years we had two more sons.

OUR FIRST GALA

WORKING WITH THE YOUTH took a lot of my time. I'd often spend all day in court waiting for a youth's case to be heard. I'd arrive early in the morning and have to go through a security search like everyone else. Too often the judge remanded the hearings and I ended up sitting around, waiting for hours. It became a full-time occupation to mentor and supervise the boys. The youth needed more time than I was able to give. I knew that I would have to quit my job in order to provide the time they required. I wrestled with the decision for a while, fearful of losing my financial stability. As a newer charity, Liberty For Youth was not receiving any funding, therefore, I was not receiving any compensation for my work. I was solely living on a dream. Much of my time was spent running to schools, workplaces and courthouses, checking up on the youth and ensuring they were doing what they needed to. I met with teachers, principals and probation officers. I attended court hearings which often took the whole day. I checked up on the youth while they worked. I knew the owners and managers hired the youth because of my advocacy. I didn't want to lose the confidence of those who had taken a risk and employed the teens.

When the youth appeared in court, I told them they needed to make a good impression and show respect. I bought them suits to wear for the occasion. I encouraged them to change their everyday style of clothing and purchased proper attire for them.

Life was intense but I realized that I was more than a mentor to the youth. I was like a father figure to them. I couldn't treat them as a number or a client. When I looked into their eyes I saw their fears, pain, and relief that someone was truly there for them. I knew my mission was to help them heal and become positive, active, members of the community again.

IN ORDER TO CONTINUE helping the youth, we needed money. Up until then, Tanya and I had been using our own funds, but our resources were depleted. We had maxed out our line of credit and were now living on overdraft. We had to remortgage our home to directly put funds into the operation of Liberty For Youth. I was basically a full-time volunteer for the organization.

I had tried raising money by going door to door selling chocolates. Every day, I strapped the kids in the stroller and went knocking on doors for 6-8 hours. I told people about my program, explaining how buying just one box of chocolate would help youth in our community. By the end of the day my feet ached and sometimes my socks were so sweaty, my feet would be sliding back and forth in my shoes.

Six months into selling the chocolates, I realized it wasn't working. I had to sell my two income properties to sustain Liberty For Youth. We personally had nothing left. I'd have to come up with a better method of fundraising. Tanya suggested hosting a fundraising dinner. I had no idea how to do that. "Just get people there and I will do the rest," she said with a wink. I looked at my wife, grateful for her kindness and tenacity. She was the backbone of much of the work at Liberty For Youth. Although employed full time at Mohawk College, every evening after dinner Tanya worked on the administrative tasks. She developed the website, designed brochures, submitted grant proposals and now planned a fundraising dinner. On top of all that, she cared for our young children while I ran program every evening.

We set a goal to raise $5,000. The night of the gala, we were shocked when we had almost two hundred guests arrive. There weren't enough volunteers and we had to request extra tables and supplies. Throughout the evening the youth involved in programming came up on stage and shared their stories. They spoke in raw form about running in gangs, doing drugs, and committing crimes. Then they shared how their lives changed once they became involved with Liberty For Youth.

Near the end of the evening, after one youth finished speaking, one of the guests walked up onto the stage and announced that he would be making a $5,000 donation. We had not publicly announced our goal to the audience. It was truly a miracle! Surprised, elated, and overwhelmed, I ran up onto the stage and embraced the donor in a tight bear hug. The gala had been Liberty For Youth's first public event and the impact had been great.

CHAPTER 5

MENTORING YOUTH

THE YOUTH WE MENTORED experienced amazing transformations. Youth from the streets, custody facilities, and courts sought our help. Parents and service providers reached out to us, too. We needed a plan to handle the influx of youth.

Tanya and I discussed what we were hoping to achieve in working with more youth. We talked about how we wanted to help youth escape their negative situations, experience freedom from their past, and embrace a second chance at life. We wanted liberty for the youth... Liberty For Youth. That would be the outreach name. We now had our charitable status, a formalized mentoring-based program model and a dynamic team of board members. I knew we couldn't operate Liberty For Youth alone. The help, expertise, and strengths of a diverse team were needed to reach more youth at risk.

The board helped me establish a partnership with the downtown Hamilton YMCA and I started running programs out of that location. The youth detention centre in Hamilton began making referrals to my programs. Approximately 18 youth were attending the programs daily.

Cliff, a volunteer at the youth detention centre, heard about the impact Liberty For Youth was making. He decided to stop by and check out our program. When he arrived, he noticed that I was struggling alone with the large group. He slipped off his knapsack and joined in to help. Cliff understood the at-risk youth. His knowledge stemmed from years of volunteering at detention centres. Cliff began assisting me on a regular basis.

During program time at the YMCA, we always met more youth to serve. I met AJ on the basketball court. He was cursing and arguing with other players. It got to the point where I had to stop the game for the safety of the other youth I was working with. I pulled AJ aside and asked him politely to calm down and stop arguing with everyone. AJ retorted angrily, "Who do you think you are, telling me what the f*** to say or do?" He told me that he had just got released from prison and that he could take out any of the guys at the gym. "AJ, I run a program for guys just released from prison. Join us!," I encouraged. He laughed and said, "No way!" However, a few weeks later he casually joined the program.

A few months later, AJ disappeared. I tried on numerous occasions to track him down, but, at every address I visited he was either kicked out or had no forwarding address. Sadly, Cliff informed me that AJ was homeless and was sleeping in parks or in bus shelters. One day as I was driving around, I happened to see AJ walking by. He told me that he had no place to go. I invited him to live at our home. AJ agreed. Within a few months, AJ returned to school and found employment. AJ's life improved and he was doing really well.

Sometimes helping youth is a matter of taking three

steps forward, then two steps back. About a year later, I saw AJ staggering around his bedroom and could hardly stand up. I looked around and noticed at least 20 empty liquor bottles. *How could someone drink so much?* In a slurred voice AJ tried to apologize and collapsed on his bed. He started crying hysterically. Immediately I thought he might have hurt himself or broken a limb. AJ then pointed at a photo taped on the wall. The photo was of a lady holding a baby. He told me that it was his mother who had died of cancer when he was a young teen. He said that since she died, nothing had ever been the same. I kneeled down beside him and just hugged him. Tears streamed down my face. I normally had an answer for the youth going through a difficult situation. Not this time. Neither of us able to speak, we spoke in the language of tears.

Tanya and I discussed the situation and thought a substance rehabilitation program might be able to better assist AJ. We looked into several options and he selected Teen Challenge. We made the necessary preparations and within a couple of weeks, Cliff and I drove AJ to Teen Challenge in London to begin their one-year treatment program. We were so proud of AJ for making this decision! On the drive home, Cliff and I felt relieved knowing that he would get the help he needed.

My knowledge and understanding of the complex issues the youth were dealing with deepened.

When I met 13-year-old Robert, he seemed beaten down from years of undue hardship. Robert's father was murdered when he was a baby and due to mental health issues and instability, his mother was unable to care for him. For a period of time he resided with a trusted friend and became a victim of sexual abuse. Robert was eventually removed from the home after becoming involved with the law. While incarcerated he felt hopeless and suicidal.

One day, Robert ripped up his bedsheets into shreds and braided the pieces together to make a rope that would support his body weight. He made a loop, placed it around his neck and jumped off of his dresser. Fortunately, the base where he had fastened the rope wasn't secure and the rope dropped to the ground.

Upon his release, Robert became a Crown ward and was ordered to reside in St. Catharines. Over the next few years, he struggled to adjust and was suspended numerous times from multiple schools. Through Liberty For Youth, Robert began completing education booklets in order to obtain his Ontario Secondary School diploma. Cliff and I would take turns driving to and from St. Catharines to bring Robert to his expulsion school in Hamilton.

Every situation was intense but none were without hope. We received a call from a community member about a homeless youth she met on a bus. We met Mohamed and took him in. He was a quiet, towering, immigrant youth whose family left him and crossed the border to the USA. He had never informed Tanya and me about the outstanding charges against him. We were downtown one day when the police stopped us. I learned only then that the boy had many unresolved criminal charges against him from across the border, as well as in Canada. The officers arrested him immediately.

When I visited Mohamed in jail, I asked why he never told me about all the charges before we had taken him in. He broke down and told me. "I needed the help and I was afraid if you knew about all my charges you wouldn't bother with me."

Sensing the boy was sincere, I bailed him out as if he was our own son and laid out a plan of care for him. Mohamed was shocked that I was still willing to help him. He had been living in fear but once he came clean, his demeanour relaxed. Grateful for the help, he followed the Liberty For Youth program conditions. In a year, he was back in school, volunteering in the community and holding down a job. Tanya and I still remember his animated laugh and joyful spirit. He also joined our Prodigal Sonz program, a basketball team comprised of at-risk and post-incarcerated youth and their mentors. The team plays annually against the Hamilton Police All-Star Basketball team led by Sgt. Barry Mungar (a former NBA player.) This event invites the community to witness and support the youth demonstrating our program's principles of respect and reconciliation with the police.

DURING ONE PARTICULAR GAME (pictured below), a large, bulky officer grabbed a rebound ball and took a step to dribble it when he glanced up at one of the Prodigal Sonz players. His mouth dropped open. "Mohamed? Is that you?"

The referee blew the whistle repeatedly and called out, "travelling, travelling," trying to get the game moving. The officer just stood there holding the ball and staring at the boy. For a few moments, the game went silent as the youth and the cop seemed to be in their own world.

"Yep, it's me," Mohamed responded with the brightest smile. He recognized the cop too. He had been one of his arresting officers. The last time the officer saw Mohamed, the boy's appearance was unkempt and his attitude was harsh. Now, clean shaven and smiling, his appearance had softened.

"Man, you cleaned up. I knew you could do it. I'm so proud of you." The officer grabbed Mohamed's hand and shook it. Realizing something paramount was happening on the court, the referee stopped the game. The audience watched unable to hear what was being said, but they sensed the moment was powerful. The interaction between Mohamed and the officer was the highlight of the game.

CHAPTER 6

A WORLD WITHIN A WORLD

SOME OF THE YOUTH who came into our home had outstanding warrants. I always encouraged them to turn themselves in to the police. It was difficult for them to do, but I always accompanied them down to the station and waited until they were processed.

One time a youth named Justin, who had read about Liberty For Youth in the local newspaper showed up at our program asking for help. He brought the *Hamilton Spectator* article with him and begged me to help him. He had a warrant out for his arrest. I promised to help him on the condition that he would turn himself in. As a surety condition, Justin would need to stay with Tanya and me. Around that same time, one of the youth staying with us had moved out of our home to attend college. Tanya and I discussed not taking any additional youth for a while as our family was growing. We now had three sons and more space was needed. We had recently cleaned the unoccupied room to use as a playroom for our sons. But after praying together, Tanya and I felt Justin found us for a reason. If he was willing to change, we would make the sacrifice.

Shortly after moving in, Justin began sneaking girls into the house. We had spoken to Justin on numerous occasions about our rules. "Rules are like guardrails, there for protection," Tanya explained. But it continued to happen. One evening we could hear whispering and giggling from the basement. Tanya calmly but purposefully picked up our nine-month-old son and went downstairs. I stared at her wide-eyed wondering what she was going to do. Tanya held up our baby in front of Justin and the partially clothed teen girl. With fire in her eyes, she asked, "Do you want one of these?"

Justin hung his head. The girl looked away. Tanya passed the girl her clothes and coat and whispered, "You are better than this. Go home." As the girl left, Tanya shifted her focus back to Justin. "Because I care about what happens to you, every night I will sit in front of that door to remind you of these loving rules," she firmly said.

He yelled at the top of his voice, "Everything I do, I mess up. I don't know how to follow rules. My mom never had any. I just don't know what to do." Tears rolled down both of their faces. In a soft voice Tanya assured him, "It's ok. We can teach you. Just let us, ok?" That was a turning point for Justin. Justin felt Tanya's sincerity. From then on, Justin's attitude changed and he began abiding by our house rules. He even began try- ing to fix things around the home.

Program participant Marcel, was beaten and bullied while incarcerated. One of the inmates promised to protect Marcel but only if he supplied him with drugs. Every time Marcel was freed, he would commit a petty crime that would land him back in custody. Again and again, I attended court hearings for the teen, not understanding why he was constantly in and out of lockup. It took 18 months until Marcel finally told me that he was sneaking drugs back inside because of the threat on his life. In his world, he was doing what he needed to do to stay alive. Once I became aware of how Marcel was being manipulated, I was able to help him.

It was like a plot in a movie. The reality of Marcel's situation exposed the depravity faced by the youth. The gangs provided youth with easy cash and lots of it. Most of all they promised safety. The pull to embrace that lifestyle was strong.

When I visited the youth in lockup, it bothered me to hear them talk about what was important to them. They had no desire for a better life. I stared at the strong, smart, and powerful teenagers as I cried inside, *They have so much potential!* This is tragic. I saw in them athletes, physicians, photographers, teachers, technicians, business owners, politicians, officers, writers, sons and fathers. They all could make something wonderful with their lives and the world around them. Instead, the teens hoped that when they got older they would share a cell 'upstairs in the jail' with friends, uncles, brothers or even their own fathers. My heart grieved. When I was their age, I dreamt of owning a car, impressing beautiful girls, and earning my own money. But they lived in a completely different mindset – a world within a world. In their world, everyone had given up on them and they had given up on themselves. I began to see that the problem was systemic.

PARENT ENGAGEMENT

TO FULLY HELP YOUTH turn their lives around, I would need to work with their parents, also. Most of the youth were from single-parent homes and 85% of them were fatherless. Many of the single moms did try to become involved, but of course, it was difficult juggling the family responsibilities alone. In an effort to help, we developed a parent engagement program. When I approached the parents and asked them to participate in the program, some expressed gratitude. They were thankful for the help and additional support. Others, however, became defensive. Some had drug addictions, mental illness, or other debilitating issues that made it difficult for them to utilize the support we offered.

An amazing mother makes her 10th year parent engagement commitment to Liberty For Youth

Working so closely with the youth and experiencing their stories gave me insight as to why youth did chaotic things. They were genuinely responding to dysfunctional circumstances. I remembered when Andrew was referred to us at just 15-years-old. His mother kicked him out after her new boyfriend moved in. Subsidized housing only allowed a limited number of inhabitants. Her boyfriend was abusive and she felt scared to ask him to leave. In her desperation, she felt telling Andrew to leave was her only option. It was just another example of how the youth had been forced to fight, forced to survive, forced to make it on their own. I knew hurting people hurt others and that Liberty For Youth was often times a last hope for these youth.

In a few cases, parents even resented the help given to their teens. When Shane graduated high school, Liberty For Youth offered him a scholarship to attend college. His mother however was not pleased. She wanted him to find a minimum wage job instead. One day, when I went to pick up Shane for the program, his mother came running outside waving a crowbar in her hand. I jumped back into the van and jerked the vehicle into reverse to get away. She swung the bar smashing the passenger side window, undeterred by the teen who was sitting there. Thankfully, the seat was reclined, and the youth suffered no injuries.

I frantically continued driving in reverse for a few blocks trying hard to keep my passenger and bystanders safe. Shane's mom continued to chase me down the street. A neighbour witnessing the incident called the police. When the officers arrived and the woman had calmed down, her son, in tears, begged me not to charge his mother. I didn't press any charges, but the incident stunned me.

I couldn't believe the mother's anger was a result of

Liberty For Youth's encouraging her son to follow his dreams. In her world education was a waste of money. She wanted him to work, earn minimum wage, and give her money. As I reflected on *a world within a world,* I prepared to tell Tanya what happened to our van window. After this incident, I decided to remove the logo to ensure Tanya and my children would be safe and not singled out for any future altercations.

CHAPTER 7

ENGAGEMENT, ENCOURAGEMENT, EMPOWERMENT

I THOUGHT BACK TO when I was young, lost, and alone. What was it that helped me to turn my life around? The teacher had engaged me in education. The police officer encouraged me with hope for my future. Tanya had empowered me with the truth to take action and heal from my past. They didn't judge me. They didn't force me to do anything. They simply gave me a choice to decide on a better way to live my life. I was, in fact, the forerunner of Liberty For Youth. I had walked the journey from brokenness to wholeness.

Now, we were reaching the youth in the same way. We met them at the point of their need and accepted them just as they were. Sometimes I brought food. It was amazing how happy a simple pizza could make them. Other times I helped with their homework. They loved it when I played basketball with them. Relationships developed. They started to ask for favours. Could I give them a ride to school, help them get groceries, or even attend a parent-teacher interview? I made sure I was available whenever and however they needed me. I understood firsthand how difficult it was for them to think beyond their immediate needs. When someone is hungry, all they can think about is food. When someone is homeless, all they can think about is where to sleep that night.

All the programs at Liberty For Youth are provided free of charge and it is up to the youth whether or not they participate. I never demanded anything of the youth and always gave them the right to choose what they wanted. I wanted them to understand that everything they did was a choice they alone were making. If they didn't make a choice, life would choose for them. Their indecision was a decision. I wanted them to understand they themselves chose their own future.

To make good decisions, it was important for them to have self-confidence. However, many of the youth lacked self-assurance. Over the years, it had been chipped away and they needed positive experiences to gain it back. They needed to accept a timeless truth: Young people are resilient and if they are determined to do something, no one can stop them.

Every so often, someone would ask me about our motto *'Giving Youth the Liberty to Choose.'* "What was the choice? What were they choosing?" My answer, "Anything and everything in life; gangs and drugs or education and work. The success of any youth lies in their decision to choose. They have the right to choose education versus incarceration. They have the right to choose creativity versus crime. They have the right to choose faith versus fear. It is their choice alone to make. We provide the tools and resources but ultimately, it's the youth's decision as to how they will live." Liberty For Youth empowers youth by giving them the freedom to choose.

So, we would help the youth choose positive alternatives by giving them new tools and resources. The more I thought about the concepts; *engagement, encouragement, and empowerment,* the more I identified those as the core principles for real change and the pillars of Liberty For Youth programming. We were already executing the elements of each core principle but now we would standardize the framework to our program.

PILLAR ONE: ENGAGEMENT

WE INVITE YOUTH TO be active participants in the program, identify their true needs and pursue them with a strong level of commitment. We relentlessly provide options and solutions to involve them in their restitution. We do this by offering transportation, food, and a place of belonging. This is similar to how the teacher supported me.

The program started with me visiting youth in detention centres. After release, I would pick up youth up in my personal four-door sedan and transport them to programming. Now with four program vehicles, Liberty For Youth staff pick up youth who are enrolled in expulsion schools, on conditional house arrest, on probation or being released from custody and bring them back to the centre. We provide meals at the centre and at off-site programming locations. A counsellor and tutors are available at Liberty For Youth one day a week.

PILLAR TWO: ENCOURAGEMENT

AFTER THE YOUTH FINISH their meals and tutoring, Liberty For Youth staff provide a ten-minute life lesson similar to what the police officer did for me. We also expose youth to new experiences and opportunities through field trips, tours, special speakers, and out of town excursions. This allows them to see and dream beyond their current situations and circumstances. Youth are encouraged and assisted in developing a strategic life plan and provided a mentor to speak hope regularly into their life.

PILLAR THREE: EMPOWERMENT

WE OFFER YOUTH RESOURCES to implement their strategic plan. We give them the tools to take action and change their own lives. If they want employment we help them draft a resume. Then they submit their resumes to businesses. If they want to get back into school we coordinate a meeting for admission. We help with bus tickets or transportation if needed.

A big part of Empowerment is having the youth own their mistakes and take action. They need to tell the truth about their behaviour and reconcile with those they have hurt when possible. Liberty For Youth provides a means to do this through Reconciliation Bursaries. The youth are offered work at our centre. They earn restitution money which is given to those they have stolen from, or whose property they have vandalized. In some cases, the youth write an apology letter. The most important thing is to help the youth understand how their actions create victims and impact lives. Then they can take responsibility in order to move forward with their lives.

The Power Of A Changed Life Gala –
Youth Scholarship Awards Ceremony

OFFERING SCHOLARSHIPS

I WORKED TIRELESSLY WITH youth at risk designing programs that would impact their lives for the better. To empower the youth even more, Liberty For Youth set up a scholarship program. Any youth who successfully completed the program and did not re-offend would be awarded a scholarship to attend college, university or an apprenticeship program. The intent was to entice the youth to stay away from crime and to take steps towards a better future.

Liberty For Youth launched the scholarship program in 2007. Clay, the first recipient to receive a scholarship, used the funds to attend aviation school. The second scholarship went to Danny. He used the money to attend a trades program at Mohawk College.

Top: Becky, a local teacher, tutors our youth weekly
Bottom: Old Navy volunteer, Josephine, tutoring our youth

CHAPTER 8

ESTABLISHING A PLACE
OF BELONGING

A LOCAL TEACHER WAS impressed when she heard that I was giving scholarships to post-gang members. She kindly nominated me for the 2008 ME to WE Award, for my part in making positive changes for youth.

At the ceremony, when I was called up to receive the award, the crowd applauded and cheered. I felt overwhelmed by their support. It was the first time my work was validated at a national level. I stood there, taking it all in and felt appreciated and encouraged. I was pumped to go back and work even harder.

The award also gave Liberty For Youth much needed exposure. More financial donations and community support came in which helped keep the program running smoothly. Then in 2010 we received pilot project funding from the Department of Justice Canada which helped shape the scope of Liberty For Youth programming. Our time now could be spent focusing on helping youth and not worrying about how to pay operating expenses. The three years of project funding allowed us to hire four full-time staff and we were able to fundraise to offer more scholarships to youth who success-fully completed the program.

Our volunteer base grew to 150 community members. People were seeing the positive impact our program was having on youth and wanted to help.

In 2011, Member of Parliament, David Sweet, nominated me for 'Canada's Top 40 Under 40' Award. This award honours forty Canadians under the age of forty for their exceptional accomplishments in five categories: vision and leadership, innovation and achievement, impact, growth and develop-ment, and community work. Being in the 'Top 40 Under 40' signified that my leadership was validated. Here I was among some of the top leaders in the country and recognized as one of them. This was important as a new non-profit leader in establishing my credibility and trustworthiness. Back at home, I received a few job offers as a result of the 'Top 40 Under 40' Award. As tempting as some of the offers were, Liberty For Youth was my passion and more youth were turning to us for help.

As the Department of Justice Canada funding was coming to an end, World Vision Canadian Programs began funding the development of our Bright Choices program. This program extended our reach to even more youth. We would reach out to youth at risk of dropping out of high school and those with mental health issues. Research told us that for a program to be effective, it needed to run three times a week. This was no surprise to us as we often spent over ten hours a week with each youth already.

One evening Tanya asked me for a 'tea' meeting. When she requested that, I knew it would be a serious conversation. She started by saying, "Over the past eight years, we have taken 13 youth into our home. We have four staff coming in and out of our basement office. Volunteers assemble here. Donors meet us here. Youth visit us here. Our children knock on the door to find us during meetings. We can hear their little feet running up and down the halls, dodging the babysitter, while we deal with situations that are sometimes a matter of life and death."

SHE PAUSED BEFORE SHE continued. "This isn't the right place anymore. We are running out of space. The youth deserve a vibrant, designated place to belong," she appealed.

I nodded in agreement. She was right. We need a building to meet the growing demands of Liberty For Youth. We

Tanya & Frederick Dryden, with their four children

had reached our limit as to what we could offer in our small 700-square-foot home plus the basement. In order to assist more youth from the community, obtaining an appropriate building was vital. It would be a youth centre where the youth could feel valued and accepted. I met with the Liberty For Youth Board of Directors and cast the vision. The Board agreed that a larger building was necessary to accommodate the needs of the youth and the increased administration.

I began looking around the city for a suitable location and saw a building I thought would be perfect. To make this possible, I'd need $70,000 for a down payment. At that time, Liberty For Youth could only afford to put $40,000 towards a building purchase; leaving us short $30,000. My mentor, MP David Sweet, connected me to Ron Foxcroft, a local business-man and philanthropist who was best known for manufactur-ing Fox 40 whistles. I made plans to meet with him. Although I had not previously met Ron, I shared my heart for the youth and our need to purchase a building. I asked Ron if he would help me start a campaign – thirty days to raise the remaining $30,000.

Ron listened to my request attentively. He paused for a few moments before inquiring, "Why me? We've just met." I proceeded to share with him a vision that I'd had on three separate occasions prior to our meeting. While I was praying about the building purchase, I saw Ron's face and knew that I needed to meet with him. Ron was astounded after hearing my answer and thoughtfully responded, "Give me two weeks to think about this."

Two weeks later, I received an email asking for me to return to Ron's office. He had discussed the proposal with his wife and they decided that they wanted to get on board to help the youth in our community. Ron had carefully set out some guidelines for the project. "Frederick you must contain your expenses. We need to raise the entire amount to pay off the building in full, so you will never have to worry about paying rent and making a mortgage payment. Let's begin a campaign that will not only raise the down payment for the building but will cover the entire cost of the building." I tried to contain my excitement as Ron spoke, this was above and beyond my initial request and would greatly impact Liberty For Youth's future.

Ron continued on with his thoughts, "Assembling the proper Campaign Cabinet is now our focus. Once the money is raised to pay for the building entirely, we must take the amount that would be destined to a mortgage payment or rent and direct it 100% to Liberty for Youth programs. Frederick, it is important that you focus on sustainability to keep the programs vibrant and healthy. Your wonderful staff will focus on short term challenges while you remain focused on long term sustainability. Our donors need to understand that we have financial stability over the long term."

I was elated. With Ron's leadership, in just under a year we not only raised the $30,000 down payment, but we went above the goal and raised $300,000 to complete the purchase.

Liberty For Youth was now a physical location. We would be a beacon of hope to the community. Having a building allowed us to more than triple our program participants. We now had a safe, co-ed space to launch a female program. This was a heart cry for Tanya and me. We could also utilize our volunteer resources more productively. The building was spacious. It was an old, but well-known, used bookstore in the east end of Hamilton. It was a fixer-upper and needed plenty of work to turn it into a space where the youth would

Frederick and Ron Foxcroft

Stelco funds Liberty for Youth to obtain a youth centre

feel welcomed. In perfect timing, the Ontario Trillium Foundation awarded Liberty For Youth with a large capital grant to renovate the centre. Renovations were completed two years later. Having a beautiful space for youth programming maximized program hours. Less time and money were spent driving to the various community centres where we hosted programming. Programs were now centralized. We began to offer consistent tutoring. We were able to offer more internships to college and university students. Youth attendance increased. Instantly, they owned the environment. The main floor was modern and monochromatic for a quiet and less stimulating experience. Downstairs was vibrant and pulsated with multiple textures, colours, and multiple seating areas for sensory preference. The music studio and kitchen were youth favourites. There was a space for everyone to enjoy.

THE DOUBLE-EDGED SWORD OF FUNDRAISING

WE HARDLY HAD TIME to celebrate the renovations of our new youth centre. Success in the non-profit sector can be bittersweet. Our building was now paid for and we were receiving funding from a large, stable organization. Everything was going smoothly. Then, unexpectedly, incoming donations slowed down and monthly partnerships decreased. Maybe people assumed that we no longer needed individual donations. To make matters worse, I received a phone call from our major funder. They acknowledged our success but they needed to end our funding as a result of them changing their mission focus.

I sat stunned. How could this be possible? Now we had a building, but no money to run programs. The funders had just recently talked to me about expanding to two other cities. They had told me that they liked what Liberty For Youth was doing; how it gave youth hope and helped them break from destructive lifestyles into productive and satisfying ones. I struggled to understand how we could work so hard to make such an impact on the lives of young people, only to have the funding cut.

Tanya and I had sacrificed ourselves, our home and our family. By this point, 400 youth had gone through the Liberty For Youth program. Our team had developed strong relationships with the youth.

I now sat in the basement and cried for these young people, even fearing for their lives. I buried my head in my hands. *Why now?*

My thoughts drifted back to how I became the founder and Executive Director of Liberty For Youth. My team of dedicated staff and I were making an impact on the lives of broken and lost youth in the city of Hamilton. I was distraught. We would have to reduce programming hours at our new facility. I sensed this would have devastating outcomes for our youth.

CHAPTER 9

THE IDEA TO RUN FOR YOUTH

SHORTLY AFTER THE FUNDING was cut, a youth named David, who had been with Liberty for Youth for three years, was fatally wounded in an altercation. His transformation had been amazing during the time he attended programming. Liberty For Youth had given him a scholarship to attend Mohawk College. He lost his life only one month before he was set to attend classes.

Another youth who had seen the Liberty For Youth van, ran over to us and begged for help. Gangs he once affiliated with were after him. Due to the funding cuts, we had reduced programming hours and were adjusting schedules. So, we referred him to another agency; but he never went. Two months later he was shot and killed in the North End of Hamilton.

The loss of these young lives hit me hard. I knew something would have to be done to keep our programs running consistently. No gaps in programming. No break in schedules.

An idea suddenly came to me. I'd hit the road running and donate my legs to the two boys who died. I would do my best to ensure this never happened again. I considered the 100 youth Liberty For Youth was currently serving. I would be running for their lives! I'd run from Ottawa (the Capital of Canada) to Hamilton (my hometown) telling as many people as I could about the youth who needed help to turn their lives around.

In order to achieve sustainability for programs we set a goal to raise $650,000 over the course of a three year campaign. In search of a new campaign chair I approached Sharon Clark, the community relations manager at the Hamilton Port Authority (HPA). Although it did take some convincing, Sharon ultimately accepted the role as campaign chair to help the youth, recognizing and believing in the important work Liberty for Youth was doing. With Sharon as campaign chair, HPA launched a donation matching initiative that would match up to $25,000 donated by Port Partners. The initiative ended up raising $50,000 for Liberty for Youth and was one of the first big donations the campaign received.

Excitement built up in me. I'd do it. I'd run for the youth who needed me – I would be their voice in action. The Liberty For Youth Centre had stood as a beacon of hope for youth, their families and the community.

A myriad of ideas began circling in my mind. I'd run to raise the money needed for program sustainability. I would *Run for Youth*.

This would be a huge undertaking and I needed to put the idea before God. If God was for the Run, I knew that it would all come together.

I LAID OUT SEVEN objectives and asked God to confirm each:

- Raise $150,000 in initial sponsorships
- Determine the route
- Obtain partners that would be committed to the vision and stand with me
- Determine dates
- Find a qualified trainer to train me to run marathons; as I was a beginner
- Obtain a reliable driver and team
- Train without serious injury

Answers to those conditions started to unfold. Sponsorships began coming in. I was ecstatic!

I mentioned my idea to two of my mentors, MP David Sweet and retired Hamilton Chief of Police, Glenn De Caire. Both had knowledge of former routes and helped me develop an actual route. Once we had a course outline, my running team and I drove the length of the route four times to pray over it and to assess the layout of its landscape. The latter was done because I needed to prepare myself for the varied terrain. We surveyed the land and made note of all one-way streets, uphill and downhill roads, and flat roadways. We also inquired if construction would be taking place during the time of the run. We wanted no surprises.

We met with local partners and asked for their support in providing speaking engagements, accommodations, funding, or support of the city mayor. We developed a concept entitled the *Mayor's Challenge* which invited mayors along the route to walk or run one kilometre with me when I passed through their city. Twelve mayors in cities along the route agreed to participate.

We designed the *Run for Youth* with purpose and intention. I focused all my energy on the youth and what they needed. Our team strategically used the SWOT method (strengths, weaknesses, opportunities and threats) to obtain information on relevant youth issues in every stopover city. The team and I met with city mayors along the route to determine their current youth-related challenges in their particular areas.

We discovered that high teen pregnancy rates, unemployment, homelessness and drug usage were common issues faced in the various cities.

The city of Oshawa asked me to participate in a round-table meeting which would take place during the run. They invited the *Run for Youth* team, together with local stakeholders for youth: the police, politicians, and community groups. They would share concerns, as well as solutions. I was extremely grateful for the opportunity because I wanted the representatives in every city to see that I was concerned with the youth needs specific to their areas.

Our team would meet with the Ontario Provincial Police and local police services along the route, to show our appreciation for their services and reconcile at-risk youth with law enforcement. When we ran through each city, 19-year-old Luis, a youth runner, would present MVP Police Officer awards to the local officers for their work with youth in their communities.

A PLAN STARTED TO take shape. The *Run for Youth* would begin at Parliament Hill on October 14th, 2016 and I'd return to the Liberty For Youth headquarters on King Street East in Hamilton on November 4th, 2016

The dates were decided for a number of reasons. Running in cool weather was ideal, because if too warm, it could cause dehydration, and if too cold, we could encounter winter snow storms. I also needed to be back in time to complete the final ten kilometres in the Hamilton Road2Hope Marathon on November 5th, to run with those in the community who were supporting me. And on November 8th, I would speak at our annual "Power of a Changed Life Gala" where guests who backed Liberty For Youth would be in attendance, including politicians, stakeholders, and local members of the community.

It was decided. I would complete a three-week run from Ottawa to Hamilton. I'd run seventeen days, and a total of 650 kilometres to raise $650,000.

Before I started, I'd speak on Parliament Hill. I would tell those gathered about the youth who needed a helping hand to help free them from the pull of the gangs, prison and drugs. I would tell whoever would listen about the need for youth encouragement and mentoring, something the staff of Liberty For Youth and I had been doing for the past 12 years.

Because I wasn't a runner, I desperately needed a trainer. Someone qualified who could get me to the point of running long distance.

Dr. Mark, a Liberty For Youth board member, started to casually train me. After I completed my first five-kilometre run, Dr. Mark drafted a letter to Esther and Gord Pauls, owners of The Runner's Den, informing them about my upcoming run and asked if they would be willing to donate a pair of shoes to me. At the time, I didn't know it, but Gord Pauls, an accomplished runner, triathlete, and triple Ironman, would accept the role as my trainer.

After I received the free pair of shoes, I wrote a thank-you letter to the Pauls, but instead of mailing it, I decided to stop by their store and personally deliver it. While there, I gave two tickets for Esther and Gord to attend our upcoming

November gala.

During our 2014 "Power of a Changed Life Gala," one of the youth shared how his life turned around because Liberty For Youth helped him break the cycle of crime and homelessness. When he finished speaking, I presented him with a ring, shoes and a coat symbolizing that 'a prodigal son had returned home.'

After hearing the youth speak, Esther approached me and said she'd like to become more involved. She went on to tell me that Runner's Den would donate $10,000 towards the run and that Gord would be willing to train me for long distance running. I was grateful for their generosity and support. God was answering my prayers!

One thing was still needed — a safe and reliable driver, someone mature and wise. Someone who had skills in medical emergencies, nutrition and logistics. Someone who could offer the help and support that I'd require over the three-week journey. A few youth had volunteered for the position. As touched and grateful as I was for their offers, I needed someone with more experience.

A year prior to the run, George, a friend of mine, who had been living in Montreal, recently retired and returned to the Hamilton area. We both attended a mutual friend's birthday party. George asked me if I needed any help at Liberty For Youth because he'd like to volunteer. I thought to myself he would be the perfect route manager and driver for the *Run for Youth*.

I was well known at Liberty For Youth for pursuing people and motivating them to get involved. Now here was George, asking me, if he could volunteer. My eyes twinkled and my smile widened. He had no idea what I was about to ask him.

I knew that George had not only been a principal, but

also a high school coach who was familiar with sports-related health issues. I immediately asked if he'd be willing to be my driver. George didn't hesitate with his answer. He said yes. One more confirmation had been fulfilled.

There were other 'miracles' that happened as well. People, from different service providers, stepped up to partner with Liberty For Youth. Six hotels along the route donated their services. Restaurants and supporters agreed to prepare meals for them. Physiotherapists and chiropractors offered their services and support and called their colleagues along the route to look out for the team.

TRAINING FOR THE RUN

FEBRUARY 2016, AT AGE 44, I aggressively trained for my upcoming run in October. For two weeks, I ran hard. Four days a week. Ten kilometres in the morning. Ten in the afternoon. My set goal – 80 kilometres a week and 240 kilometres over three weeks.

However, 14 days in, after completing 160 kilometres, my body hurt badly. My ankles, red and swollen, throbbed terribly. Even after I iced them, the excruciating pain didn't subside.

I had started training for the long-distance marathon convinced I could do it. Most of the things I attempted in the past, turned out successfully. This would be no different. I was confident that I could manage the long-distance marathon. I was blessed with good health, good genes, and although I was never a runner, I had played sports in school.

Now I wasn't so sure. I rubbed my legs trying to relieve them of the agonizing pain, but the throbbing wouldn't stop. I started to wonder if I should give up, but to quit the run meant giving up on the youth who depended on me. They needed me and I had promised I wouldn't let them down.

I clenched my jaw and thought about the two boys who died and all of the other youth we were helping. I knit my brow with determination. I could not, would not give up. I dropped to my knees and begged God to help me. "I can't do this. The pain hurts too much. I know you wanted me to complete this *Run for Youth*. Help me, God. Please help me." Then a Bible verse popped into my head – Romans 9:16: "So then it is not of him that wills, nor of him that runs, but of God that shows mercy."

The words played over and over in my mind until I finally realized that I had been trying to do this in my own strength. I went before my wife, the board members, the campaign team and the youth, and confessed that I had been proud. As the words fell from my lips, relief washed over me.

Afterwards, I laced up my runners and continued to train. This time I knew I wasn't running alone or in my own strength.

After I ran every kilometre, I quoted, "So then it is not of him that wills, nor of him that runs, but of God that shows mercy." Those words pumped me. Made me strong. Gave me power. More than that, once I admitted and confessed my pride, and realized God was in the run with me, I suffered only a few minor injuries – pain in my left knee, bleeding from chafing and blisters on my feet. Moving forward, I found a new strength to bear the pain and continue training while continuing to perform my Executive Director duties at Liberty For Youth.

CHAPTER 10

THE LAUNCH

DAY ONE

OCTOBER 14, 2016 — THE official launch day for the run had arrived. People began gathering on Parliament Hill where the opening ceremonies were set to take place. As I scanned the crowd, I saw many partners of Liberty For Youth, the Deputy Mayor of Ottawa, other dignitaries, sponsors and young people. Seeing them all overwhelmed me. I squeezed Tanya's hand, grateful for her presence beside me. She was my rock, my strength and greatest supporter. A twinge of sadness passed through me knowing I wouldn't see her or my children for the next few weeks. The fear of not being able to finish the run, being injured or not being able to play with my kids again crossed my mind. Having the support of so many people helped dissipate my anxiety and the adrenaline kicked in.

At three o'clock, the master of ceremonies, Hamilton's

Top: Luis, Frederick and Cliff Simon on Parliament Hill
Bottom: Frederick, the Youth Panel, and many generous sponsors

local Member of Parliament, Bob Bratina, welcomed everyone to the event. The band played, people cheered. Nervous energy ran through me. I watched as the youth panel took their positions at the front.

Based on the SWOT analysis research conducted prior to the run, our team discovered Ontario had a lack of youth voices. We decided it was essential to start the launch hearing from young people themselves. Youth representatives from various groups such as the Indigenous community, African/Canadian community, LGBT community along with other diverse backgrounds and cultures spoke about the *Run for Youth* initiative and how they felt.

One youth panellist named Dada said, "Collectively, I believe our voices were heard because of how diverse the panellists were, with different minds and experiences – we were able to relate to the majority of the people there."

During the run from Ottawa to Hamilton, awards would be presented to deserving youth who had either moved away from conflict with the law or who had completed an academic achievement. Each would receive a large plaque bearing their name and a $250 bursary. The purpose was to recognize these individuals and inspire youth in their communities. At the launch, each youth panellist was presented with a Canadian flag while their accomplishments were highlighted. The first award and bursary were then presented to one of the youth panellists.

When it was my turn to speak, I had my speech all ready, but as I gripped the microphone and looked out at the people present, I felt touched by all those gathered. Too overwhelmed and nervous, I couldn't get my words out. I kept thinking to myself, *Oh my gosh, the day is here. It's finally here. We're doing this!*

I glanced over at Luis and handed him the microphone. Luis was celebrating his nineteenth birthday that day. Pride swelled in me as I looked at the teen. Luis had been with Liberty For Youth for six years. He was recommended to the centre by his lawyer and probation officer. Back then, he was full of anger and in constant trouble with the law. His life now had completely turned around. Additionally, Luis had been friends with one of the boys who died and asked if he could do the run with me in honour of his buddy. Although he wouldn't run the full 650 kilometres, I was grateful for him being there, running with me and now speaking for me.

My desire has always been to empower youth and I had prepared Luis in advance to speak at the launch. It was important to me to have a youth be the one to share the final remarks, be a voice for the younger generation and launch the run.

After speaking, Luis and I took our starting positions. The master of ceremonies started the countdown. When he shouted, "GO," we took off running. The crowd cheered and hollered encouragement.

Dada, the youth panellist who had been given the award ran along the walkway to the gates of Parliament, shouting, "Go Frederick. You're doing this for all of us. You can do this."

The youth's presence stirred up a myriad of emotions in me. I knew that he ran out of gratitude. My vision to turn around the lives of youth was making an impact. It humbled me.

Luis and I ran through the streets of Ottawa. As our feet continually hit the pavement, I felt invigorated and apprehensive. It had been a gruelling preparation. Hundreds of hours spent in planning and training. Any pain I felt now would be because of the actual run, and not for the run. The wind blowing softly on my skin, and the brilliant sun shining down on me was a delight. It felt like I had been let out of a cage. It was the exact freedom that I wanted for all youth to experience.

The kickoff was exactly how I imagined it – magnificent. Now, I was finally doing this! I ran with purpose and hope. I ran for the youth, to change their lives for the better. I wasn't alone. The support and encouragement from those behind me inspired me to stay the course.

One of the major corporate sponsors, RBC Royal Bank of Canada (RBC) had a request. They asked me to speak at thirty-one branches along the route. RBC Career Launch student, Michael, contacted the banks and arranged for all the speaking engagements prior to the run.

Within the first few minutes into the run, I stopped at an Ottawa branch to speak to them for five minutes (pictured below). It thrilled me when I saw the staff outside cheering, waving flags and holding water in their hands. Altogether, I stopped at four RBC branches that day. At one of my stops, a youth named Bobby from the Indigenous community,

who had served on the youth panel at the launch, said he was inspired by the opening speeches. He asked George, our driver, if he could run with us for a while. Dressed in jeans and normal attire, Bobby ran ten kilometres with Luis and me. He ran with passion and confirmed to me that my efforts were already reaching youth.

As the launch ceremony had ended in the late afternoon, we were only scheduled to complete ten kilometres that day. When it began to get dark outside, the team and I headed back to the hotel.

I was still feeling overwhelmed by the day's events. The day had been emotional, so much so, I could hardly speak. The magnitude of what I was doing hadn't fully hit me yet. I thought about all the people who had come up to me on Parliament Hill and said, 'What you're doing is amazing.' Tourists and groups wandering by the event stopped and expressed their awe when they learned more about my mission. The day rolled over in my mind as I drifted off to sleep.

DAY TWO

THE FOLLOWING MORNING, I woke up at 4:00 a.m., did some stretches, and then hit the road at 4:30 a.m. I ran 11 kilometres before I returned to the hotel at 6:30 a.m. I stretched, iced my sore muscles and soaked in a hot bath before eating a good breakfast. At 8:30 a.m., I ran another 11 kilometres before returning to the hotel at 9:30 a.m., to prepare for my upcoming speaking engagements.

The previous day's jitters had left me. I felt good running. I was back in training mode. From 12:00 p.m. to 2:00 p.m. I ran ten kilometres. This was the first time that I had to myself since the launch.

As I ran, emotions overwhelmed me. I had always wanted to do something for the youth, something tangible, something real. It hit me hard that this *Run for Youth* was me advocating on behalf of the youth, something I could personally do for them. Tears streaked down my face. The thought that I was making an impact on young lives completely humbled me.

I thought of my own life and how a teacher, a police officer, and my wife had impacted me. They not only showed kindness but had connected with me in a way that touched something deep inside my core. I wanted to do that for youth everywhere. I wanted them to know they were not alone, that someone cared, that I cared. Whenever I saw a youth hurting, lost or broken, I wanted to reach out to them. I knew from experience it could take months or years for them to open up, but I wanted to be in their lives for the long haul. I wouldn't give up on them like those who had never given up on me.

I thought about the phone call I received, informing me that the funding had been cut. I remembered thinking, how could they cut off funding when our programs were positively impacting lives? It had felt like a surgeon began an operation but then midway through decided not to finish it.

Discouraged, I had prayed and prayed and prayed asking God to show me what I could do to keep the doors of Liberty For Youth open. The Sunday morning after I learned of the funding cuts, I sat in a church pew hoping to hear something that would provide an answer. Pastor Shanna spoke about the call of God on someone's life and about the uncertainty and the sacrifice involved. She talked about Abraham and Moses and how they had used their feet to fulfill a purpose – advocating for those in bondage and seeing lives changed. At the end, she pulled out a map that showed the route one of the men had taken over his journey.

I didn't make the connection that day. A few days later, I pulled out the map Pastor Shanna had shown. Then, I took out the potential route for the run from Ottawa to Hamilton. I put the two maps side by side and then turned my map upside down. Her map and mine were in exact alignment. Together they made a full circle. Chills ran through my body. This was the confirmation I had hoped for; a direct sign that I needed to undertake the *Run for Youth*. I knew I'd use my feet to make a difference.

Now here I was doing it. The run was a statement of what I could do for our youth. Our youth need assistance and mentorship on a consistent basis. I would not give up on them regardless of the ups and downs of funding. I thought of the two precious lives lost while we transitioned between program funding. I knew there were other influences that led to their untimely deaths, but I still wonder if additional programming hours would have kept them safe. I was running so that our programs would not solely be dependent on third-party funding guidelines and disbursement schedules. After running ten kilometres, the van picked me up to allow some time to rest before I completed another ten kilometres. I finished the later run, now on the outskirts of Ottawa.

DAY THREE

SUNDAY, I WOKE UP at 4 a.m. and completed my usual routine before hitting the road at 4:30. I had finished 32 kilometres by the time I reached the town of Morrisburg, where I had a speaking arrangement set up. After my talk, Luis presented a

Most Valuable Police Award (MVP) to Morrisburg Constable James Blanchette. He was so touched by the gesture and what we were doing, that he asked me if I would speak to some local high-risk youth on Tuesday. I agreed, knowing this would affect the route schedule and would require me to begin my daily runs earlier than planned.

Before I completed my last run that evening, Michael wanted to return to Ottawa to say goodbye to a friend. He, Luis and George dropped me off and promised to return to pick me up in an hour and a half. At the last minute, I decided to give my cell phone to them, as I wanted to run light and unencumbered.

I ran five kilometres before conducting a brief speaking engagement in a small community. This community had a lot of animosity towards youth issues related to law enforcement in the area and I felt compelled to address this matter. After the brief speaking engagement, I continued to run. I noticed it had begun to get dark, and there were no lights on that particular section of the route. I was feeling a little worried at this point. I kept running, wondering where on earth George was. I noticed a car in the distance slowly following me for about fifteen minutes. Suddenly the car pulled up beside me and rolled down the passenger window. The man inside called out to me, "Hey, I noticed you running. You look awfully tired. You want a ride?"

I waved him off, "No thanks. I'll be alright." I told him.

The man continued to talk to me. "It says Liberty For Youth on the back of your shirt. So what's Liberty For Youth?"

I glanced over and noticed a couple of bottles of water lying on the car seat. I needed to drink. I had completed approximately 100 kilometres over the past three days. I was exhausted and my body was sore and dehydrated. The invitation to sit down and rest was tempting. I reached to open the car door, but as I did, I remembered the rule of the run, *Never under any circumstance take a ride from a stranger.*

I pulled back. The whole thing seemed fishy. "No thanks," I told the man and kept running. The man waited for a few minutes before driving away. It was now quite dark and there was no one else on that stretch of road. Fear played in me as I ran in the dim moonlight. Suddenly, in the bushes beside me, I saw the glowing eyes of coyotes staring back at me. In a panic, I quickly crossed the road to give myself some distance from them. *Where was the van?* My body was in so much pain but I ran from fear of the man in the car returning and the coyotes nearby. My hips started hurting badly and from my training experience, I realized that I must have passed the designated meeting point and still my team was nowhere to be found. I had no way of knowing where they were and had no way to contact them. There was not a house or store in sight, just complete darkness. Now limping, I made the decision to turn back and head towards the hotel. As I was jogging, a vehicle sped past me and then quickly braked. I strained my eyes to see the vehicle in the darkness and then immediately heard a familiar voice call out to me.

Relief swept over me when I recognized George's voice. I answered him and slowly limped over to the van. I crawled into the back, stretched my legs out and gulped down two bottles of water. I lay back grateful to be off my feet, but feeling somewhat agitated I asked, "What happened? Where were you guys?"

They told me that traffic had been stalled because of an accident on the highway and they couldn't get through. Knowing this was a factor beyond their control, my agitation subsided and the mood lightened. I felt grateful to be safe and reunited with the team.

I ran a total of 47 kilometres that Sunday, five more kilometres than planned. Back at the hotel, I iced my sore body. I was completely exhausted. While I soaked in the tub, the reality of the run set in. I was feeling the pain and still had 19 days to go. Tanya had told me that I needed to take time off from running each week. I felt relief that I listened to her advice. Tomorrow would be a 'rest' day. I would use these run-free Mondays as Media Awareness Days. I was passionate to present findings from our SWOT analysis and be a voice for the youth.

DAY FOUR: MEDIA AWARENESS DAY

I WOKE UP MONDAY morning feeling refreshed after a good night's sleep. Thinking about the awful pain I was in last night, I was grateful for the reprieve. However, the day would be a full one, with five speaking engagements scheduled. The first speaking engagement at a local high school began at 9:00 a.m. I spoke to the students about the *'Prevention'*[1] of youth issues such as youth unemployment, high school dropout rates, crime and incarceration. I stressed the importance of addressing these various factors before they turned into serious problems. I also informed the students that every $1 spent in prevention, saves $17 in taxpayers' money.

Afterwards, at 11:00 a.m., I called into the Bill Kelly CHML

---

[1] *Dooling, Anjana. "Crime prevention pays: Why stopping crime before it happens saves us all." Crime Prevention Ottawa: Ottawa. 2009: https://onwecottawa.files.wordpress.com/2014/05/crime-prevention-pays.pdf*

900 Hamilton radio program to update my local followers. I shared my passion for youth and updates of the run. At noon I spoke to the Brockville Rotary Club and at 5:30 p.m. I shared my vision with the Ottawa Metro Rotary Club. Unfortunately, time didn't permit for the fifth speaking engagement.

Oftentimes, when I shared my message along the route, I felt emotional, remembering my own painful past. A few times, I couldn't finish speaking. During these moments, Luis and George would conclude the message. People really connected with my message since the issues were relevant and current. They understood why helping youth was important in their communities.

The first Media Awareness Day went extremely well. I received several standing ovations and many Rotarians gave donations to local youth initiatives. Others gave donations to Liberty For Youth. It thrilled me to see that people were hearing, receiving, and acting on the message. The *Run for Youth* gained awareness through Social Media. Additional requests poured in asking me to attend more speaking engagements. Knowing people were acting on my message, I was even more determined to lace up my shoes over the next few weeks and run the remaining 600 plus kilometres.

CHAPTER 11

BLOOD, SWEAT, AND ICE

DAY FIVE

MY SPEAKING ENGAGEMENTS INCREASED from 49 to 72 appearances. Due to the added talks, we had to make changes to my run schedule. The only way we could make it work for the remainder of the run, was for me to complete 21 kilometres before breakfast; instead of my usual 10. Before I set out, I ate and drank nothing to avoid bathroom breaks and during that time, I stopped only to stretch and drink water.

Our team was set to move to a new hotel after I finished running 21 kilometres that morning. The hotel owner had told us that if he had vacant rooms available, we could stay free of charge. When I completed my run and we arrived at the next hotel, the parking lot was full of trucks and there was no vacancy. I continued my scheduled speaking engagements for the day, but we would have to return to Morrisburg that evening.

As arranged by Constable Blanchette, who had received the MVP police award a few days earlier (pictured below), I went to speak to a few high-risk youth at a local middle school. However, when I arrived at the school that morning, the principal asked if I would be willing to speak to a larger group of students instead, at an assembly.

Hundreds of kids piled into the auditorium. Luis spoke as well. His story was powerful and relatable to the youth. Luis impressed upon the students that police officers were friends, not enemies. He then presented the MVP award to Constable Blanchette for a second time, but this time he did it in front of all the students.

AFTERWARDS, A 10-YEAR-OLD girl approached me. She thanked me for coming and hugged me. It left me thinking how important children are and how much of an influence we have in their young lives. I realized again that people were depending on me. I promised myself I wouldn't let them down.

After I left the school, I hit the road and ran ten kilometres before I gave another talk to bank employees. I then ran another six kilometres. Afterwards, I headed back to the hotel in Morrisburg and took a hot bath before my final run of the day. I poured a large amount of Epsom salts into the water without thinking twice.

The previous day, on my visit to the Rotary Club of Brockville, a Rotarian named Josh Bennett had asked to run with me for my last five kilometres into Brockville. Josh organized the media to be present while I gave a speech at the 'Welcome to Brockville' sign (pictured below).

I had to stop every few kilometres as Josh and I ran because I was feeling dizzy and faint. Josh became concerned and asked if I was alright, but I dismissed it as nothing. Later that evening, when I related to Tanya what happened, she told me that the effect of too many Epsom salts being added to the bathwater combined with the increased distance of my morning runs had caused dehydration. It was the reason I felt light-headed. Experience is a great, but tough, teacher.

Top: Brockville Chief of Police, Scott Fraser receiving MVP Police Award on behalf of Constable Mark Heffernan. Bottom: RBC — 2459 Parkedale Ave, Brockville with Frederick and Luis.

DAY SIX

ON WEDNESDAY MORNING, AS our next hotel accommodations had been overbooked, our team had to wake up extra early to drive 60 kilometres back to Brockville, where I had finished the evening before. I ran half a marathon and then we all drove back to the Morrisburg hotel to check out. In our attempt to make checkout time and arrive at my next speaking engagement on time, I forgot some of my clothing and other personal items. I also had no time to compress, ice or stretch.

As I ran towards Gananoque, I thought about the results of the SWOT analysis. I wanted to ensure I properly conveyed solutions in each city I ran through. When I ran, I felt alive and free. I was one with my body and mind. It was when I had my best prayer times. Every step I took was an accomplishment. A step closer to the next speaking engagement. A step closer to Hamilton. A step closer towards helping youth. A step closer to soaking in a hot bath.

Every time I laced up my runners, I thought about the youth who would benefit from the run. The run was a way I could advocate on their behalf and not turn any more youth away in the future.

The run was not only bringing awareness about the needs of youth, but it was also helping me heal from my own painful past. Running gave me time to reflect. As my feet continually hit the pavement, I thought of all the times I had struggled to make it from one day to the next. Thoughts of being locked in the dirty basement, the cockroaches and the abuse made me cringe.

As these haunting memories played over in my mind, I pushed them from my thoughts. I felt grateful to now be in a position to prevent youth from being trapped in similar situations.

I completed one kilometre, then another and another. With each completed kilometre, the throbbing in my legs increased and blisters formed on my feet, but the pain in my body didn't equal the discomfort of how I had lived as a teen. As I ran, I realized I was using my past to push others forward. Even more so with each kilometre, I knew I was empowering youth to make good decisions like I had made.

CHAPTER 12

THE RHYTHM OF REALIZATION

DAY SEVEN

DAY SEVEN BEGAN IN Gananoque. I ran a total of 42 kilometres and conducted two presentations; one at the Rotary Club in Kingston and the other, during a radio interview in Gananoque.

Today was a good day. While running, I kept a steady, rhythmic pace. I felt my heart pumping hard, and my legs moving in sync, one with the other as my feet hit the pavement again and again and again. I felt strong and unbeatable when I ran in a rhythm. By using a steady pace, I could master my tolerance for pain and hardship. Staying in a flow helped me focus on my goal instead of the throbbing and exhaustion.

TEACHING FINANCES

In hindsight, I realized my strong work ethic pushed me to

make sacrifices in order to realize financial independence and take control over my life. Money or lack of it determines much of what one can or cannot do in life. So, when I developed programs for Liberty For Youth, I pulled from my own personal experience of working my way out of being a street youth.

Teaching finance to the youth was important because the way they handled money was affected by their scarcity mentality. I also knew that the youth we served tended to wrap their identities in money. Gang members made large amounts of cash stealing and dealing drugs. For them, it was a business. Their lifestyle appeared successful, but in reality, it was highly stressful and costly.

Financial lessons proved essential. More than once, we had calls from concerned mothers after they found astonishing amounts of money in their sons' bedrooms. Tanya received one of these calls after a mom found a shoebox filled with $10,000. One of the lessons Liberty For Youth often teaches is *easy come – fatally go.*

Clay struggled with this "easy" income as well. He left three times in the four years he stayed with us. The third time I cried when I found him. I tried to persuade him to come back home. Clay shoved his hand in his pocket and threw a roll of cash at me. It hit my chest with a thud. It felt like a punch. I couldn't even imagine how much was wrapped up in there. "Can Liberty For Youth give me this?" Clay challenged. "I can't even get a job. There's no way I can make this kind of cash the right way." Heartbroken, I returned home alone. I couldn't force him. I hoped that my time with him, teaching him the power of good choices, would wake him up to the serious consequences wrapped up in that deadly roll of money. Thankfully, he returned a few weeks later and never ran away again. He wanted to do life the right way. He wanted to earn an honest living.

As I worked with youth, I also realized they had little or no knowledge of money management. Many were in debt and turned to criminal activity to pay back the money they owed. I taught them about basic finances using a practical step-by-step approach. The principles included earning a legitimate income, budgeting, credit and debt payments, savings, investments, diversifying (giving back), and wealth management.

The lessons focused on the value of honest, hard work. I taught them how I bought my two homes on a salary of $35,000 a year, while at the same time providing for my daughter. For the youth who wanted to learn more, I provided detailed material on real estate investments using myself as an example of how I made sacrifices and worked long hours. Clay called recently to thank me for encouraging him to read the financial books when he resided with us. He told me that he had originally hated reading them, but now at 30 years of age, he sees the value. The knowledge from the books positioned him to buy his first home.

MOST OF THE YOUTH never had a bank account. We set up a fund to start each youth off with $100 and partnered with local banks to assist them in setting up their first no-fee bank accounts. It would be their first step toward connecting with financial institutions. However, I soon realized a number of the youth had no identification. Some didn't want any. They wanted or needed to stay anonymous. For others, their parents had lost the documents or had to leave them behind in a crisis situation. I explained how it important it was to have identification in order to obtain employment, receive a paycheque and establish credit for their futures. Without identification or credit, they couldn't purchase or own anything legally.

I told them they could use the skills they learned from selling drugs and being involved in crime to start a legitimate business. We taught the high cost of being involved with drugs and crime. That troubled lifestyle was filled with anxiety. There was the unsteady income, unsafe environments and the very real possibility that at any moment that they could be injured or killed. Bottom line — yes, the gangs offered money, exciting possessions and a sense of belonging, however, it was not what it appeared to be. Crime had nothing to do with being truly successful or sincerely loved. In a gang, their lives were controlled by a bunch of unstable individuals who think youth lives are dispensable.

CHAPTER 13

THE DRAMA OF A DREAM

DAY EIGHT

BY THE EIGHTH DAY, our team was now staying at the Ambassador Hotel in Kingston. The hotel had graciously given us complimentary accommodations.

Early that morning George drove me to the outskirts of Kingston to pick up the run where I had left off. This stretch of the run was paramount. Once I made it into Kingston, the first week of the run would be completed, with 240 kilometres behind me.

I ran the 21 kilometres towards Kingston in a rainstorm. I was soaked and realized I needed to increase my body temperature to avoid getting cold and sick. To diminish the absorption of the cold and rain, I ran at a slower pace for the first five kilometres. I then increased my pace at ten kilometres, again at 15 and also at 18. As I increased my speed, my body temperature increased but my right knee began to throb.

I was grateful to see people around when I finally made it into the city. I greeted anyone that crossed my path. Two blocks from the hotel, I passed a physiotherapist's office that was open. By now my knee was hurting badly, but I was sweaty, soaked and dirty. I didn't think they'd treat me in that condition, so I kept running, but the pain was excruciating. I turned back and went in to ask for help.

When I walked into the office, I learned the staff had heard about the *Run for Youth*. They told me that someone from my team had called their office a few weeks ago requesting donated services. When the associate made a call to the owner, she told them to provide treatment to me at no cost and asked me to return later that day as she would personally like to meet me. Relief and gratitude swept over me.

When I returned, the doctor spent an hour with me trying to determine where my pain was coming from. She finally concluded it was mechanical. One of my legs was shorter than the other. She told me that I had trained well and had the muscle mass to do the long-distance run. However, she taught me how to augment my run style so that I could make it to Hamilton without experiencing the agonizing knee pain again. This was one of the many acts of kindness that I experienced along the way.

My stopover in Kingston was one of many highlights of the *Run for Youth*. Tanya and the boys met me there and I was able to spend time with my family.

Frederick's rainy arrival into Kingston,
Kingston City Hall ›

DAY NINE

THE FOLLOWING DAY, I had scheduled a non-running day so I could focus on the Indigenous youth in the area and present awards to those who fit the award criteria. Our team spent most of the day north of Kingston in a small town called Sharbot Lake, where an Indigenous community was located. Sharbot Lake was not on the route, but it was intentionally chosen in advance. Bobby, who had served on the youth panel in Ottawa, met us there as this was his hometown.

Shari, who taught in Sharbot Lake, understood the people and the challenges they faced. Shari nominated two youth to receive the bursary awards: Kat, a 17-year-old who had suffered a lot of abuse and 13-year-old MJ, who had also been through a lot of struggles in his young life (pictured below).

In the evening Liberty For Youth hosted a musical concert. The First Nations Women's Dance group performed, to everyone's delight.

After the performance, MJ was presented with a $250 bursary and a plaque of achievement. MJ was so overwhelmed, he went outside to get some air. I followed him to see if he was okay. He told me, "It was the first time anyone has ever given me something like that." I understood what he felt. This is why I detoured to Sharbot Lake. In fact, this was why I was running.

Kat was also presented with a $250 award & plaque. I promised her that if she was accepted into college, Liberty For Youth would provide her with a scholarship.

Later that night, the team returned to the hotel in Kingston feeling fulfilled. The visit to Sharbot Lake had been wonderful. It was great to spend the day celebrating the Indigenous culture and heritage (pictured below and on the following page).

CHAPTER 14

FROM RUNNING TO FIGHTING

DAY TEN

OCTOBER 23RD WAS A moving day. These days were always hard on me. I ran 21 kilometres from Kingston to the outskirts of Napanee. Afterward, George drove me back to Kingston where I spoke at the West Side Christian Reformed Church on the topic, *The Good, The Bad & The Ugly of Mentoring*. While speaking I started to feel extremely tired and nearly fainted. I was forced to abruptly end my message. I'm sure they understood my fatigue.

After the church provided lunch for our team, George drove me to a second speaking engagement at an Old Navy store north of the city. Later, I changed from my suit into running clothes. When I exited the change room, everyone laughed because I looked like Clark Kent ducking into a phone booth and coming out transformed into Superman (or as my youngest son called me, 'Mr. Running Man.')

I hit the road and continued to run another half marathon. In the afternoon, I met with the Ontario Provincial Police and we presented them with an MVP award.

DAY ELEVEN

TODAY WAS A MEDIA and awareness day focusing on 'Intervention.'[2] First thing in the morning, I shared my story with the youth at a local high school. I called in to the Bill Kelly radio show afterwards to give updates on the run. I then spoke to the Belleville Rotary Club at 12:00 pm. At 2:30 p.m. I had a radio interview with a Napanee radio program. Later that day, I spoke at an RBC branch in Napanee. I shared with my partners that it can cost anywhere between $63,000 to $95,000 provincially to incarcerate one youth aged 12-17. For a chronic young adult offender, it can cost up to $280,000 annually on a federal level. In contrast, one year of programming at Liberty For Youth serving 100 youth costs $700,000; therefore, saving millions in taxpayer dollars for every individual that is kept out of the justice system. Intervention is extremely necessary, as 74% of institutionalized adults were once youth in conflict with the law. These facts gave my audiences a better understanding of why reaching out to youth is vital and empowering them to become more involved.

[2] *The Monetary Cost of Criminal Trajectories for an Ontario Sample of Offenders, Koegl, 2011: https://www.publicsafety. gc.ca/cnt/rsrcs/pblctns/mntry-cst-crmnl-trjctrs/index-en.aspx*

DAY TWELVE

ON OCTOBER 25TH, I ran from Napanee to Shannonville starting at 4:00 a.m. George always drove five kilometres ahead of me because it motivated me to run the distance to catch up to him. That particular morning, while running my first five kilometres to reach George, I heard loud barking. When I reached George, I asked him to keep an eye out for coyotes. George drove only one kilometre ahead this time. It was a good thing he did!

While waiting for me, George spotted a coyote, then two, then a whole pack. In a panic, George spun the van around and drove back to me. "Get in the van," he shouted. "Get in the van!"

I dove into the van quickly. George told me he had seen the pack of coyotes ahead. After that, we decided that George, from then on, would only drive one kilometre ahead.

Once in Belleville, the team checked into the hotel while I continued to run. A Mississauga donor attended the Belleville Rotary meeting with Petra, a Belleville resident who is a friend of his. She was so inspired, that to support me on the run, she organized a community-friendly boxing

In Belleville, Frederick gave Aaron Reinert his best shot

event with youth. While sparring with the youth, I discussed concerns and issues with them. It was a wonderful opportunity to hear what the youth had to say and get a few jabs in! It's important that adults know that youth just want to be listened to and understood. This is the best way to connect with youth, at-risk or not.

In the afternoon, youth from Quinte Christian High School, where I had spoken the day before, met with me at The John Howard Society. A group of youth were gathered to run the last five kilometres with me. For me, it was a powerful time to connect with the young people and their explosive energy invigorated me. It was the first time in a while that I ran pain-free.

At the end of the day, Petra invited our team to her home for dinner. She had been following the run and felt that we all needed a good home-cooked meal. It was the best food we had eaten since the run had started. The family atmosphere and the delicious meal lifted our spirits. Petra did for us what we aspire to do for the youth: Create a safe, normal place away from the pressures of life.

A Belleville police officer signs the Run For Youth map

DAY THIRTEEN

THE FOLLOWING MORNING, I completed the partner day run in Belleville. I ran around the perimeter of the city, something I had also done in Kingston. The partner days allowed me to connect with new supporters, conduct additional speaking engagements and present youth bursary awards in the cities we were passing through. While running that day, I somehow missed the cut-off.

I didn't see George and the van waiting for me so I continued running another three kilometres. As I continued, I realized I was running out of the city and had not seen Quinte Mall where George and I had agreed to meet.

Finally, I stopped, crossed the street and went into a local business to call George. A man sat inside reading a newspaper. He looked up and smiled at me. "Would you like a drink?" he asked. "Sure," I answered. The man pointed to a water machine. I gulped down the cool liquid and then asked if I could use the washroom. The kindly man nodded. When I returned, the man said, "You must be lost. Would you like to use the telephone?"

I was shocked and wondered, *How does he know I'm lost?* As if reading my mind, the man lifted up *The Belleville Intelligencer* newspaper he had been reading to reveal a large photo of me along with an article about the *Run for Youth* from Ottawa to Hamilton. The man had known all along who I was and that I had gotten far off my route. After a quick laugh, I used the phone to contact George to let him know where I was. This was yet another act of kindness that enabled me to keep going.

DAY FOURTEEN

THURSDAY, OCTOBER 27TH WAS a moving day for our team. I woke up at 3:00 a.m., ran half a marathon, ate breakfast, packed up my stuff and checked out of the hotel by 10:00 a.m. My first speaking engagement that day was in Brighton at the Beacon Youth Centre. There I presented Blake, an Indigenous youth, with a $250 bursary and a plaque for his achievement in completing high school despite the adversities he'd faced (pictured above).

Afterward, Brighton's Mayor Walas met with me at the Beacon Youth Centre to complete The Mayor's Challenge. He walked with me through the city to an RBC location in support of the run. A run was scheduled at the Trenton Military Base at 5:00 p.m. later that day, but we got a call informing us that some changes were made and the run would need to be at 1:00 p.m. instead. There was no time to check into the hotel or eat lunch. I didn't want to miss the run with the

military, so after my walk with Mayor Walas, I immediately went straight to the military base.

When I arrived, I was in awe of all the young men and women in the military that were warmed up and ready to run the agreed three kilometres with me. The commander shouted in a thunderous voice, "Let's get going!"

We took off running (pictured above). I ran behind the commander. As we entered the base, around fifty military men and women stood cheering and clapping. I thought we had finished the run, but then the commander belted out that we would circle the base, "One more time!"

I was exhausted. These were paratroopers who were trained and prepared for drills. The speed they ran at tired me out, but I was grateful for their support and enthusiasm. I did another lap around the base with them. Although we were originally supposed to run three kilometres, we ended up running five instead. I left the military base with a newfound respect for the athleticism of those in service to our country.

DAY FIFTEEN

I STARTED MY MORNING running 21 kilometres. I met with Cobourg Mayor Brocanier to conduct The Mayor's Challenge. Following our meeting, I spoke to the local Cobourg Rotary Club. Afterwards, I ran another 21 kilometres. The Port Hope police station was our next stop. We presented the MVP Police Award to the entire detachment, as their inspector felt it was necessary to honour their team collectively for their youth engagement in their community.

DAY SIXTEEN

DAY 16 STARTED LIKE the rest of my days. However, arrangements were made for me to meet with a group of incarcerated youth at Brookside Detention Centre between my runs. When I arrived, memories of when I had visited Barton Street Jail in Hamilton came flooding back into my mind. When I first started speaking, the youth seemed uninterested and disengaged. However, by the time I finished speaking, I was amazed at the questions they were asking. Some of the youth inquired how I overcame my troubled past as they also wanted to turn their own lives around, get an education and contribute positively to society. I was so touched that I made a commitment to offer scholarships to those who followed through. The youth were so overcome by the gesture that some began to break down. When I saw their reactions, I decided to gather them all in a circle and I concluded the speaking engagement with a prayer. Today was a special day for me as it reaffirmed the exact reason I started Liberty For Youth.

DAY SEVENTEEN

AFTER RUNNING 21 KILOMETRES, I arrived in Bowmanville, where I spoke at Liberty Pentecostal Church. Later that day, I was greeted by Mayor Foster, who proclaimed October 30th as Youth Declaration Day. Mayor Foster's support embodied the very purpose of the *Run For Youth* mission; to bring awareness to youth issues. This day was one of the most exhausting, yet uplifting days of my journey.

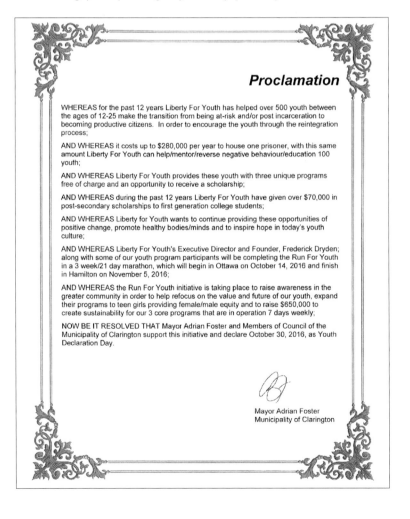

Proclamation

WHEREAS for the past 12 years Liberty For Youth has helped over 500 youth between the ages of 12-25 make the transition from being at-risk and/or post incarceration to becoming productive citizens. In order to encourage the youth through the reintegration process;

AND WHEREAS it costs up to $280,000 per year to house one prisoner, with this same amount Liberty For Youth can help/mentor/reverse negative behaviour/education 100 youth;

AND WHEREAS Liberty For Youth provides these youth with three unique programs free of charge and an opportunity to receive a scholarship;

AND WHEREAS during the past 12 years Liberty For Youth have given over $70,000 in post-secondary scholarships to first generation college students;

AND WHEREAS Liberty for Youth wants to continue providing these opportunities of positive change, promote healthy bodies/minds and to inspire hope in today's youth culture;

AND WHEREAS Liberty For Youth's Executive Director and Founder, Frederick Dryden; along with some of our youth program participants will be completing the Run For Youth in a 3 week/21 day marathon, which will begin in Ottawa on October 14, 2016 and finish in Hamilton on November 5, 2016;

AND WHEREAS the Run For Youth initiative is taking place to raise awareness in the greater community in order to help refocus on the value and future of our youth, expand their programs to teen girls providing female/male equity and to raise $650,000 to create sustainability for our 3 core programs that are in operation 7 days weekly;

NOW BE IT RESOLVED THAT Mayor Adrian Foster and Members of Council of the Municipality of Clarington support this initiative and declare October 30, 2016, as Youth Declaration Day.

Mayor Adrian Foster
Municipality of Clarington

DAY EIGHTEEN

ON MONDAY, MY DESIGNATED media day, I arrived in Oshawa where Mayor Henry had prepared a roundtable meeting (pictured below). Those in attendance included Durham police officers, a Durham College representative, a group from the John Howard Society, advocacy groups for the homeless, youth representatives and other politicians from all levels of government. We met together to discuss youth issues and advocate for them. My primary goal was not only to raise money for Liberty For Youth but to raise aware-

ness of the issues and concerns related to young people. I spoke on the topic of *'Retention.'* I shared how when staff are not retained, or there's a high level of staff turnovers, there is an increase in youth abuse and neglect.[3] Financially it costs about 20% every time there is a staff change, due to training and administration.

DAY NINETEEN

AFTER RUNNING THROUGH PICKERING, we drove back to Bowmanville to speak with the Bowmanville Rotary Club (pictured below) and at an after-school program. Following my speaking engagements, I returned to the Scarborough area to continue running. I found a new sense of energy as I began to see signs for Toronto, but I soon realized that Toronto was a lot further away than it appeared. When I finally reached my destination, I was so thankful to God for giving me the energy to finish a challenging day of running.

---

[3] *The Cost of Employee Turnover: https://www.peoplekeep. com/blog/bid/312123/employee-retention-the-real-cost-of-losing-an-employee (August 2013)*

DAY TWENTY

ARRIVING IN TORONTO WAS an emotional highlight for me. This partner day included seven speaking engagements. One of the places I visited was the Jane and Finch Community Centre (pictured below and to the right). This was the same neighbourhood where my friend Vince was shot in grade nine. Memories flooded back of when I wandered these same streets as a youth, believing I'd never achieve anything.

Here I was back on these same streets now advocating for youth. It was important for me to tell them that there is hope for their futures. I gave out two bursaries that day; one to a youth who completed high school, the other, to a student who had chosen to go on to college.

DAY TWENTY ONE

THURSDAY MORNING, I DEPARTED Toronto and ran along the route towards Etobicoke. When I reached Mississauga, I spoke at the Credit Valley Mississauga Rotary Club, where my good friend, Paul, a Rotarian, welcomed us. After departing, I ran to a Mississauga RBC branch and spoke to those who had gathered. Later that evening, some friends from Hamilton drove up to see us. It felt great to see some familiar faces and know that the end was in sight.

CHAPTER 15

COMING HOME TO HAMILTON

DAY TWENTY TWO

I WOKE UP EARLY Friday morning in Mississauga (see photo on the preceeding page). I was aching to get home. My body hurt and I longed to see Tanya and our children. Instead of running my normal 21 kilometres, I pushed myself to do 30.

I eventually made it into Burlington and saw familiar streets and signs which motivated me to keep going. I was almost home. I kept going, my adrenaline pumping me to go faster, longer. My emotions up one minute, down the next. I had made it to Joseph Brant Hospital and considered running on the QEW to arrive home sooner. I just wanted the run to be done. I was too hyped, and knew I needed to calm myself down. I turned around and ran back to Burlington's City Hall, in order to release the built-up adrenaline. Along the way, people recognized me. They pointed and shouted, "You're the guy running."

At City Hall, I spoke to the gathered crowd before I headed back for my 9:00 a.m. speaking engagement. Michele Bailey, owner of Blazing The Agency, generously donated $10,000. Additionally, Michele pulled other people on board to back me, including the former Mayor, Ann Mulvale, of Oakville and representatives of the ever-supportive RBC Royal Bank.

I had three more speaking events, but since I was ahead of my run schedule, George encouraged me to run another six kilometres, a total of 36 kilometres that day. It would mean I'd only have six kilometres left for my run to the Liberty For Youth centre. I agreed and ended my second run at 2:00 p.m. at Hutch's restaurant on Van Wagner's Beach Road in Hamilton.

That afternoon I met with Burlington Mayor Rick Goldring at a local RBC branch, where he declared November 4th a National Youth Day. He was the second mayor to make such a declaration. Liberty For Youth serves many youth from Burlington and Mayor Goldring's youth activism encouraged me.

When I stepped outside afterward, the streets were packed with cars. Sadly, there was a fatality on the Skyway Bridge and traffic was backed up everywhere. I needed to reroute my run and George wouldn't be able to drive me to the designated run spot.

The Corporation of The City of Burlington
Office of The Mayor

PROCLAMATION

Whereas   **Liberty for Youth** has helped over 500 youth between the ages of 12-25 to make the transition from being at-risk/post incarceration to become productive citizens by encouraging, mentoring and coaching them through the reintegration process; and

Whereas   incarceration costs can amount up to $280,000 annually per youth. This same amount can help mentor, rehabilitate and educate up to 100 youth; and

Whereas   **Liberty for Youth** provides at-risk youth with unique programs free of charge, as well as an opportunity to receive a scholarship; and

Whereas   since its beginnings, **Liberty for Youth** has granted over $70,000 in post-secondary scholarships to these first generation college students; and

Whereas   **Liberty for Youth** strives to continue providing youth with opportunities for positive change, to promote healthy bodies & minds and to inspire hope; and

Whereas   **Liberty for Youth** staff and program participants will be taking part in the *Run for Youth* – a three week/21 day marathon beginning in Ottawa and finishing in Hamilton; and

Whereas   the *Run for Youth* initiative hopes to raise awareness in the greater community, in order to focus on the value and future of our youth, as well as to expand programs to include teen girls and to raise funds to ensure sustainability of the core programs.

Therefore   I Rick Goldring, Mayor of the City of Burlington do hereby proclaim,

November 4th 2016 as
"Liberty for Youth Day"
in the City of Burlington.

Dated this 31st day of October, 2016

Mayor Rick Goldring

Instead of the remaining six kilometres, I would now have to run an additional eight kilometres, meaning that I would be running a total of 50 kilometres that day, more than a full marathon.

When I realized that, I didn't think twice or I may have just given up. I took off running in the direction of Liberty For Youth. My body hurt terribly. I was worn out. I pictured Tanya and the kids. I'd be home soon. Every ten minutes Tanya called to encourage me. She gave me the strength to keep going.

AT ONE POINT, TANYA told me that Hamilton Mayor Eisenberger and the local police chief, Eric Girt were waiting for me. She asked if I wanted someone to pick me up instead of running the extra kilometres, but I wanted to complete the run on foot. I'd run the full route no matter how bone tired I felt. I wanted to model to youth how to handle life when unexpected situations arise.

George, meanwhile, had managed to get the van out of traffic and pick up Luis. He rushed him over to the last kilometre run point where he'd meet up with me. Luis and I would run the last kilometre together. Amazingly, George dropped Luis off at King Street and the Red Hill Valley Parkway in Hamilton at the same time I arrived there.

As Luis and I reached Parkdale and King Street East, tons of people lined the streets cheering us on. We were welcomed by Mayor Eisenberger, Chief Eric Girt, an RBC run team, youth runners and many others. Mayor Eisenberger presented plaques to the Run for Youth team who worked tirelessly to make the run a success (pictured at top right).

After the mayor's speech, everyone ran the last kilometre with us to the Liberty For Youth centre.

I immediately spotted Tanya. I grabbed her and pulled her tight. Our youngest son held up a sign that read, 'Welcome home dad.' Many community members had come out, and to my delight, many youth were there as well. I was glad to see so many youth present. I had done it all for them.

Inside the centre, I headed downstairs to the basement and crashed out on a couch. Pain numbed some of my excitement, but lying there, surrounded by family, friends, youth and supporters, I felt tremendous gratitude and relief (pictured below).

It had been a long and exhausting day but I had done it. I

had done it for the youth, to make a difference and give them a voice. I had reached my goal; no youth would be turned away again.

The youth had seen my commitment to them. When I started the run, my biggest fear was that I wouldn't finish, but I had made it back to Hamilton!

DAY TWENTY THREE

THE FOLLOWING DAY, I finished the *Run For Youth* in the Hamilton Marathon Road2Hope. I was so touched that many supporters wanted to end the run with me. I started the day running one kilometre with children and local supporters, followed by my last, painful, ten-kilometre run. Local partners, donors, community members, family and youth were there to cheer me on.

I finished the run on Saturday, November 5th in my hometown of Hamilton, Ontario. It felt surreal to cross the finish line. I had run 715 kilometres during the run and 2,200 kilometres in preparation for the run. I promised the youth I would do it and through God's strength I had delivered.

RETURNING TO NORMAL

I HAD COMPLETED THE three-week marathon, but the runner's high was still in my system. A couple of times I woke up at 5:00 a.m. and worried that I had slept in and felt a desperate need to find George. In those moments, Tanya calmed me down and reminded me that I had finished the run. It was hard, at first, for me to settle back into my regular routine.

The Hon. Filomena Tassi, Minister of Seniors

Road2Hope co-founder, Gord Pauls

Two days later, on November 7th, my sons asked me to run around the block with them. We ran three kilometres together and when we returned, I slumped into a chair on the porch breathing heavily. My sons stared at me in amazement and wondered how I could be so tired after such a short distance.

I FELT BITTERSWEET AS I reflected on everything. Somehow, I had managed to run over 700 kilometres in three weeks and now after running only three kilometres, I was exhausted.

As I reflected on the fast-paced schedule over the past few weeks, the realization hit me that God had protected and enabled me to complete the run. On my own strength, I never could have done it. The proof was me huffing and puffing after running only three kilometres with my kids. Gratitude welled up in me, knowing that God had been with me every step of the way, helping me to physically do what I couldn't on my own. While I sat on the porch trying to catch my breath, I knew it was done now. The mission was accomplished.

The days had been a whirlwind of running, talking, and engaging strangers. I had run on a high for so long that my feelings now fluctuated between happiness and bewilderment. I felt drained, tired, and even panicky. And my body hurt. Back spasms pained me so badly that I couldn't bend down to tie my shoes. I suffered from an aggravated disc, forcing me to use a cushion to relieve the pressure.

On Wednesday evening, I spoke at our Liberty For Youth "Power of A Changed Life" gala. The Hamilton Chief of Police, Eric Girt sat at my table and noticed me trembling. He put his hand on mine to reassure me that I'd be alright. I managed to get up and speak a powerful message to the audience.

Post-run, I struggled with many emotions. The run had

been paramount in my life. It had involved scores of people day in and day out. I missed the *Run for Youth* team terribly and also the speaking engagements. Everywhere I went, I had felt loved. I took great pleasure in speaking and empowering people and having strangers pour out their love towards me. Now all of that was over. Finished. Life once again had settled into a routine, but after running on a fast-paced schedule and a daily high, routine seemed too ordinary.

For a year following the *Run for Youth*, I battled with anxiety. I often stared at my kids, feeling guilty, and wondered if I would be able to play with them again because of the physical pain in my body. My back spasms were so bad, I couldn't imagine lifting up my sons. Since the run I had put on some weight, felt physically tired and mentally drained. My physiotherapist recommended that I do no more than ten kilometres at a time. Numerous people had contacted me asking what I was planning to do next, now that the marathon was complete. Little did they know, I was just trying to survive and heal.

In time, I came back to myself. I saw that the impact of the *Run for Youth* had been huge. Many of the people I met over the three weeks stayed in touch with me. Some wrote letters. Others sent donations. All expressed their gratitude for what had been accomplished.

During the run, our team had posted daily videos and social media had taken off. The result was many wanting to know about Liberty for Youth. The phones rang constantly. The wait list of young people who wanted to go through the Liberty For Youth program was growing.

I was touched by something even greater. The youth told me they knew I'd complete the run. I remember I had even questioned myself whether or not I'd be able to do it, but the youth never questioned it. They had complete trust in me. I never knew they saw me in that way, someone who said something and followed through on it.

The youth had seen the sacrifices I made for them and what I went through, being in constant pain and having to continually drum up resources. No longer was there a sense of entitlement; now they had a better idea of what it took to operate Liberty For Youth. They had more respect, greater trust and a lot more motivation to do the grunt work.

Some of the youth who had graduated from the program and were now working and/or had started their own businesses used what they had to pay back. Some cleaned the centre free of charge; others offered landscaping and HVAC services. Most of the youth had no money to give, but they became more aware of their use of Liberty For Youth resources. They stopped wasting and started contributing what they could. They turned off the lights when they left a room and when they used a product, they finished it rather than throwing it away half used.

THE REASON FOR SACRIFICE

SINCE I BEGAN MY outreach to youth, I have considered the work of Liberty For Youth as possibly the last chance some youth might have at getting free from a destructive and negative lifestyle. I vowed to never close the door on any youth. Instead, I'll always give them second, third, fourth, and never-ending chances.

I view Liberty For Youth as giving hope to youth at risk. They are the future. I see their potential and want to plant in their hearts and minds the unlimited possibilities and dreams that they can achieve. I do everything out of love for the youth who are broken and lost.

Spending quality time with young people and speaking into their lives can go a long way. Hearing 'I believe in you' can be life-changing! One kind word could keep someone from harming themselves, joining a gang or from dropping out of school. Everything that worked in my life to help me, I use to impact the lives of the youth at our centre. For example, when I was twelve years-old and locked in the cold, dark basement for hours by myself, I started sketching to pass the time. Drawing calmed me and gave me peace. So, at Liberty For Youth, art is an integral part of the centre. The walls are full of the youth's artwork. Even the design and logo were vetted by youth.

TWO YEARS LATER

MAY 1ST, 2018, GEORGE and I re-visited the route I had run from Ottawa to Hamilton. We first returned to Parliament Hill. I sat and reflected on the powerful launch two years earlier. Tears welled up in my eyes as I remembered the many youth and supporters who had attended. In my mind, I envisioned the smiles on their faces. I could even hear the voices of the youth encouraging me.

I had been scared about running the three-week marathon, but I knew I had to do it. As I look back now, it had been much harder than I expected. I knew I couldn't do it again. The toll it had taken on me was great. Physically, it had been hard on me and I had battled strong emotions throughout the course of the run.

I reflected on why I had decided to run in the first place.

It was for the youth who, due to funding cuts, were turned away. I ran to give them a place of security, a place where they could find support and love, a place that could give them more than money could. I ran to give them a voice. I ran to inspire hope for youth everywhere. I ran for their lives.

As George and I walked the path at Parliament Hill where Dada, in his dress shoes and suit, carrying a briefcase, ran and cheered, "You can do it!" I smiled, remembering what Dada told me afterwards. "I ran with you because I truly believe in your vision. Many people dream big and have great visions but only a few can actually turn those dreams and visions into something real. You inspired me that day, just knowing that there are others out here who truly care about those who are less fortunate than the rest of us. Being someone who I look up to, I saw you as my role model and therefore, it was my pleasure and duty to run with you so that I can

continue to learn from you and stay motivated by you to do more for the greater good."

George and I walked through the streets of Ottawa and met with some of our partners. During the *Run for Youth* we had the following corporate sponsors: Old Navy, RBC Royal Bank of Canada, the Deputy Mayor of Ottawa, Rotary Club and the Hamilton Port Authority.

Afterward, George and I drove to Sharbot Lake and met with Kat, the youth who had received a bursary. We delighted in the changes she had made in just two years. Kat happily told us that she wanted to become a dental assistant. I promised we'd give her money to get her driver's licence, as there is no transportation in the area, and a scholarship towards her studies.

Afterward, we met with MJ. He greeted us grinning from ear to ear and wearing a Liberty For Youth t-shirt. In the two years, MJ had grown taller than me and was visibly more confident. He told us that he was in a grade eleven co-op and doing well. He excitedly told us his goal of wanting to become a computer engineer.

He admitted when he first heard about the run, he thought I was crazy to do it because it was such a long distance, but now, he is grateful for Liberty For Youth and the impact the marathon had on his life.

Opposite page: "Almost 12 years ago, I met Frederick Dryden. After hearing his story and seeing the life-changing work he was doing with troubled and marginalized youth, I got involved. His leadership has earned him the distinction of receiving the National Award—Top 40 Under 40. He continues to not only reach out to youth but to mentor tomorrow's leaders to continue his legacy!" —David Sweet, MP, shown with his son, Chris, as they help Frederick cross the finish line at the Hamilton Marathon Road2Hope.

George and I continued on to Brighton. We stopped by the Beacon Youth Centre to check on Blake who had been a recipient of a bursary. Blake, now working at two jobs, was unable to meet with us. We were happy to hear he was doing well!

We also met with Ray, a retired RCMP officer. Before the run, when Ray had learned what I was doing, he took a badge that the RCMP had given him for a decade of service and gave it to me as a token of his appreciation. I was so touched. This is now one of my most prized possessions.

Then we met with Mayor Adrian Foster in Bowmanville and asked why he had declared a national youth day in the city. The Mayor told us, "Liberty For Youth gets in front of causes before they become a real issue." He was impressed by our dedication and commitment to youth.

Over the course of three weeks, many lives had been touched. Those who sponsored and those who came out wanted to become more involved in making a difference in the lives of young people. Many of the youth experienced transformation in their lives. Some even acknowledged they needed to forgive others because they wanted to live free.

THE RUN HAD BEEN powerful. It created something special. As George and I drove back home, I knew in my heart the run was done and after every ending, there is always a new beginning. It was time to move forward with a new goal.

Today, I'm still running to save the lives of youth, only now, I'm running in different ways.

CHAPTER 16

A NEW VISION

MY HOPE IN COMPLETING the *Run For Youth* was to provide financial sustainability to keep the doors of Liberty For Youth open so that no youth would ever be turned away. During the *Run For Youth* we raised $350,000, which was $300,000 short of the total $650,000 goal.

Although the money helped considerably, the ongoing need to help youth at risk is great. I needed a plan to sustain the costs of impacting their lives long-term.

I would start a new campaign to provide sustainable funds called, 'Future Now.' I'd use the money from the *Run for Youth* to launch a social enterprise which would focus on three aspects:

- Sustaining Liberty For Youth programming (no funding gaps)
- Creating employment for the youth
- Sustaining Liberty For Youth for future generations

Creating jobs for youth at risk is a big challenge. Some youth have criminal backgrounds, mental health problems, and other situational hurdles. This often makes it difficult for them to secure employment. We would be able to employ the youth while earning revenues that would contribute to sustaining programming and also providing scholarships.

We considered three different social enterprise models. Purchasing an existing business was an option, however, we couldn't find a business that synergized with our future plans. Another option was opening a large community centre, but any building in the city of appropriate size would not be within our budget. Running from Ottawa again was not an option... although many people have asked.

The third option was to purchase land where we could invest literally and symbolically in the future of Liberty For Youth. It would stand for generations as a legacy by the board of directors, donors, partners, and supporters of our youth. This would be thinking past program sustainability to foster organizational sustainability. It would be a heritage for the youth. Purchasing land would be a testament to the youth and community saying, *Liberty For Youth will always be here for you and your children.* What a possibility!

Tanya has always been researching ways to improve the programs and services we offer to the youth. One day she came across an equestrian development program that was working with youth at risk in Western Canada. Two professors from the University of Regina were running a research study on how horses help teenagers overcome drug abuse. She realized this might work for the youth in our program. In fact, while I was training for the *Run for Youth*, a former board member introduced Tanya and Hanna, one of the girls in the program, to her horse. She remembered the special bond that developed between Hanna and the horse over a few visits. *To run an equine program, we would need land.* Tanya dismissed her thoughts. She had no idea that I was thinking my own audacious thoughts with land involved.

One evening, Tanya, over a cup of tea, spurted out all that she had been considering, researching, and dreaming. Equine Assisted Learning (EAL) would provide hands-on social skill development, a therapeutic environment and options for youth to work with their hands and raise funds for Liberty For Youth. It would provide a respite to those who cannot cope in our current inner-city location. Many youth who attend Liberty For Youth often have anxiety transitioning out of a destructive lifestyle with negative behaviours. Being in the rural area would reduce the negative stimuli and temptations which would inhibit progression. Breathing in fresh air, taking in the visibly open space, and feeling the calm rhythm of nature would benefit the youth. Having a rural-based program is something youth don't always get a chance to experience.

A DECISION TO BUY A FARM

TANYA CONTINUED ON ABOUT a large property for sale in Mount Hope. It was beautiful and full of potential. She was just dreaming about launching the horse program in a space like it. I told her we should go see it. She thought I was crazy, but drove out to show me anyway. Instantly I connected the dots to the social enterprise. The price was high, but I felt that burning in my heart. This could be the legacy for future generations of Liberty For Youth. *FutureNow,* my thoughts confirmed. "Yep, this is it!" I said. "Are you crazy?" Tanya said as she rolled her eyes with a nervous smile. We looked into each other's eyes. We both knew this meant work. We both knew this would be worth it, just like every other sacrifice we made. This time we didn't feel alone.

I wasted no time thinking about how I could purchase the land. I met with my Board of Directors, staff and youth. I brought them out to see the property and visually presented the idea to them. Everyone loved the vision and could see the potential for the future. Liberty For Youth put in a conditional offer.

Everything Tanya, my team, and I had done to impact the lives of youth in the city had all been done by faith. We knew the next step would be accomplished in the same way – united in prayer and agreement and motivated by faith to move forward.

Over the following weeks, I drove back to the site several times. One day, I brought my sons with me. After buying them ice cream cones, we walked around the outskirts of the property and prayed. At one point my 11-year-old stated, "Liberty For Youth is going to get the land, Dad." I tried to explain to him that it wasn't a sure thing, but he shook his head and said again, "Liberty For Youth is going to get the land!" My son's words slipped into my heart.

As I walked around the property, my heart filled with gratitude. I knew God was preparing us and now expanding Liberty For Youth's vision and outreach in such a surprising, new way.

A few weeks later, we learned our offer was approved and we could now begin the next steps of our expansion stage. The funds raised from the *Run for Youth* were used to purchase the land and the money from sales of this book will be allocated towards the development of our new equestrian program on Liberty For Youth's land.

I thought back to when I attended Tanya's church that first time and heard the pastor's words, *Who is willing to go feed the hungry? Who is willing to care for the infirmed? Who is willing to visit those in prison? Who will help the broken, the lost, the drug addict? Who is willing to go?*

I remember how those words had burned in my heart. I walked around for days afterward unable to shake the compelling need within me to do something, to reach out, to make a difference.

And when Jane in the Barton Street Jail had handed me a note saying, *You are ready to start your own program. God has given you the gift of wisdom through teaching youth,* although unsure and fearful as to what to do, I knew deep down inside, I needed to move forward. That same knowing was in me now about the expansion of Liberty For Youth.

Over the last 14 years, Liberty For Youth has made its mark in the city of Hamilton, reaching over 600 at-risk youth, helping many turn from living destructive lifestyles to productive ones. Many community members seeing the successful impact of Liberty For Youth got involved – individuals, community groups, churches, politicians, business owners, leaders, donors, partners, families, and the youth themselves. Their financial help and sincere support enabled us to keep the doors of Liberty For Youth open.

The enormity of the needs, however, is great. There are so many more youth who need to be pursued. I am ready and wanting to do more. The run, the forward pursuit, to support youth at risk is not over. I am no longer running for their lives, I now am running for their bright futures. As I prepare to embark on expanding the outreach, I know I can't do this alone.

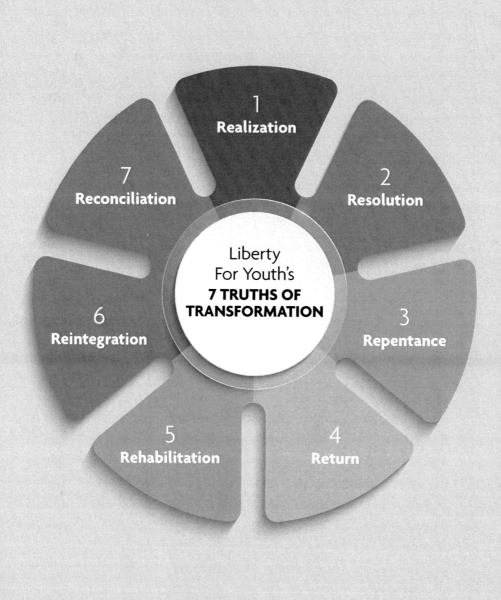

PROGRAM MODEL OF CHANGE
LIBERTY FOR YOUTH'S 7 TRUTHS OF TRANSFORMATION

Our Mentors guide the youth through various transformational stages represented by seven words starting with "R." Mentors build rapport with the youth and create a safe space for them to express their inner feelings, the good the bad and the ugly. But before any real progress can be made, the youth must first come to the (1) **REALIZATION** that he/she wants to make a change in their life.

Once that realization dawns, the youth are encouraged to make a (2) **RESOLUTION** to take action on that realization. As they start to act in new ways they are often faced with feeling of (3) **REPENTANCE** for previous behavior. Now they are truly at a turning point.

Momentum begins to build as the youth actualize their intentions and (4) **RETURN** to the mainstream. During this (5) **REHABILITATION** period, the youth are given many opportunities to accomplish things that help them to build self-esteem and self-respect.

But (6) **REINTEGRATION** is not always easy. Things don't always go smoothly. Not everyone is willing to forgive or forget the youth's past transgressions. Again, the mentor is there to support the youth, as they move into this stage of re-establishing themselves in the community.

The ultimate goal of our mentors is to see the youth experience (7) **RECONCILATION**; with themselves, their families and the community they chose to live in.

YOUTH UPDATES:
WHERE ARE THEY NOW?

LUIS recently returned home from a mission trip to the Dominican Republic. While there, he helped build a community centre and also became a mentor and sponsor for a little boy. Luis has plans to begin Bible College within the next year. His life has completely turned around and he wants to now make a difference in the lives of others.

CLAY eventually went on to Conestoga College to study aviation on a scholarship he received from Liberty For Youth. Today, Clay is a family man with two sons and has worked for the same engineering company for the past seven years. Recently, he was approved by the bank for a $400,000 mortgage to buy his first home.

MICHELLE experienced abuse at a young age at the hands of her father. Michelle's family had to leave the city they were living in and relocate to Hamilton. Michelle started attending Liberty For Youth in 2015. Since being in our program, Michelle has obtained employment and gained much needed confidence. Michelle often struggles with anxiety, but is determined to break the chain of unemployment in her home. Michelle is currently attending college on a Liberty For Youth scholarship in the field of photography and dreams of becoming a famous photographer.

ROBERT became involved with Liberty For Youth at the age of 13. He is still on a recovery journey.

DANNY graduated from Mohawk College. Danny has worked for years as a Heating, Ventilation and Air Conditioning (HVAC) Technician. He has recently started his own company in the trade and lives with his wife and son.

MOHAMED graduated high school and attended Mohawk College. Mohamed now lives in Vancouver and works in sales and business. Standing six-foot-four-inches tall, Mohamed takes pride in his appearance and only wears suits – a far cry from his once wild, unkempt attire.

GLORIA started attending Liberty For Youth programming in 2015. Gloria battled with mental health issues, low self esteem and social anxiety. Over the years Gloria has become more involved in programming and has come out of her shell. Gloria has actively trained to run with Frederick and it has positively affected her mental health. Gloria completed her first job as a summer student with Liberty For Youth in 2017. Gloria is a talented artist and is currently completing her high school education.

AJ received a Liberty For Youth scholarship and is attending Redeemer University. AJ was baptized a few years ago and is now working at Crossroads as an Intern Community Engager. AJ and his girlfriend Debra have a dream to open a mental health facility to assist youth with addictions in the future.

HANNA When Hanna first became involved with Liberty For Youth, she was involved in an abusive relationship. Hanna's experience with the pilot Equine program resulted in her acknowledging her need for help. Hanna began studying Early Childhood Education at Mohawk College. Hanna became pregnant midway through college and considered dropping out. However, with the support of Liberty For Youth she was able to graduate college before giving birth.

COEN Growing up, I would often get myself into bad situations and as a young Indigenous man not many opportunities were given to me. Since high school, Liberty For Youth has always been there for me. They continue to keep me grounded and help me take the right path in life. They've given me a brighter future by keeping me out of trouble, through their basketball program. I am now a new parent and continuing on my path to become a police officer.

WORDS FROM...

PAULO ROLO

Frederick's determination and attitude towards life inspires youth. His sincere wisdom and thoughtful approach helped my nephew David to make better choices. We are honoured that David's memory was commemorated through the *Run For Youth* initiative. My family and I will forever cherish Frederick's friendship.

CAROL DRYDEN

Frederick is my beloved brother. We have been through so much together. We emigrated from Jamaica to Canada at a very young age. We are now proud Canadian citizens. We didn't have the greatest upbringing. That is putting it mildly. We experienced a lot of mental and physical abuse. However, we somehow managed to beat the odds.

Not only was Frederick determined to not repeat the cycle of abuse, he decided to help others overcome the odds as well. My heart bursts with pride for the work that he is doing.

SHARON CLARK

Every day Frederick dedicates himself to the youth and to raising awareness for the challenges they face. This remarkable dedication was illustrated when he ran 17 marathons over 21 days from Ottawa to Hamilton — in hope of creating financial sustainability and a legacy for Liberty For Youth.

Frederick selflessly gave everything he had physically, mentally, emotionally, and spiritually to help raise awareness and provide at-risk youth with a pathway to opportunity and personal success. I hope through courageously sharing his remarkable journey, Frederick will inspire readers to be the best they can be by letting go of the past and creating the future they desire.

VANIDA HANNAN

I met Frederick back in 2005 when he came in to sell one of his investment properties to finance Liberty For Youth. I advised him that he should not sell everything and instead make long-term plans for his young family. In all honesty, I told Frederick that he was crazy.

That's when Frederick challenged me to volunteer at their 1st Liberty and Justice Unity basketball game, where the youth play against police officers. I thought, "How interesting; let's see if sparks will fly." I was wrong. I have been to most games and I have seen the bonds formed and camaraderie between the youth and the police officers.

Frederick bears the mark of a true leader, one that unites for a common cause. I am still bewildered by his energy and commitment. Frederick runs his charity with such clarity and transparency that you'll be hooked.

CLIFF SIMON

I've had the privilege to work with Frederick for over 11 years, from the time Liberty For Youth was a small outreach, operating from the basement of Frederick's family home. There are three words that capture who Frederick is: love, perseverance and sacrifice!

I remember in the early days of the ministry, Frederick approached me in confidence, sharing with me how he wanted to give up. However, just like the 17 marathons in 21 days, it was the love for the youth that caused Frederick to endure the pain and suffering, knowing it was all for them!

RUNNING FOR THEIR LIVES
INITIAL ITINERARY

DAY 1 Friday, October 14th, 2016 – Ottawa, ON
Staying at Adams Airport Inn – 2721 Bank St., Gloucester, ON
9:00-11:00 am, Media launch and interviews

LAUNCH FROM PARLIAMENT HILL, OTTAWA
1:00 pm, MP Bob Bratina, Master of Ceremonies and Amanda Kay, National Anthem; 1:05 pm, Performing Artist Melo (@VibebyMelo); 1:20 pm, Darin Martin Band; 2:00 pm, Youth Panel; 2:30 pm, Speeches from dignitaries and community leaders: Ottawa Chief of Police Charles Bordeleau; Ottawa Deputy Mayor Mark Taylor; VP, Corporate Partnerships & Community Fundraising Ottawa Senators Foundation, Jonathan Bodden; Ottawa Old Navy Manager, Evan McCluskey; RBC Royal Bank, Branch Manager, Tom Palisak; Rotary Member, Randy Reeve; Manager, Corporate Services, Hamilton Port Authority, Sharon Clark; 2:47 pm, Frederick Dryden; 2:52 pm, Moment of Silence for Youth for two youth who died senselessly due to funding cuts; 2:53 pm, Rev. Karen Dimock, Opening prayer; 2:55 pm, Photos

3:00 pm, Commence run; 3:15 pm, Old Navy 50 Rideau St.; 3:30 pm, Pita Pit 373 Dalhousie St.; 3:45 pm, RBC 139 Rideau St.; 4:00 pm, RBC 90 Sparks St.; 4:20 pm, RBC 99 Bank St.; 4:45 pm, RBC 475 Bank St.; 5:00 pm, RBC 745 Bank St.; 6:30 pm, Old Navy 175 Trainyards Drive

DAY 2 Saturday, October 15th, 2016 – Ottawa, ON
Staying at McIntosh Country Inn – 12495 County Rd 2, Morrisburg, ON
4:30 am, Wake up; 5:00-7:00 am, 1st 10.5km Run; 9:00-11:00 am 2nd 10.5km Run; 12:00 pm, Speaking at RBC #909 South Keys Shopping Centre; 1-3:00 pm, 3rd 10.5km Run; 4:00 pm Speaking at Old Navy on Bank St.; 5-7:00 pm, 4th 10.5km Run

DAY 3 Sunday, October 16th, 2016 – Winchester, ON
Staying at McIntosh Country Inn – 12495 County Rd 2, Morrisburg, ON
3:30 am, Wake up; 4-6:00 am, 1st 10.5km Run; 8-10:00 am, 2nd 10.5km Run; 1-3:00 pm, 3rd 10.5km Run; 4:30 pm, Present MVP Police Award to Winchester OPP; 5-7:00 pm, 4th 10.5km Run

DAY 4 Monday, October 17th, 2016 – Iroquois, ON
Staying at McIntosh Country Inn – 12495 County Rd 2, Morrisburg, ON
Media Awareness Day: Speaking/Teaching/Interviews
6:00 am, Wake up; 7:00-8:00 am, Physiotherapy; 9:00 am Speaking at Redeemer High School; 10:30-11:00 am, Radio Interview: CHML; 12:00 pm, Speaking at Brockville Rotary Club; 5:45 pm, Speaking at Ottawa Metro Rotary Club

DAY 5 Tuesday, October 18th, 2016 – Prescott, ON
Staying at Johnstown Motel – 1843 Hwy #2, Johnstown, ON
4:30 am, Wake up; 5:00-7:00 am, 1st 10.5km Run; 9-11:00 am, 2nd 10.5km Run; 10:00 am, Speaking at Morrisburg Public School; 12:00 pm, Speaking at RBC in Prescott – 302 King St.; 1-3:00 pm, 3rd 10.5km Run with youth to Brockville; 5-7:00 pm, 4th 10.5km Run

THEN THE ITINERARY WENT OUT THE WINDOW
My speaking engagements increased from 49 to 72

DAY 6 Wednesday, October 19th, 2016 – Brockville, ON
Staying at Comfort Inn – 22 Main St. Gananoque, ON
4:30 am, Wake up; 5-7:00 am, 1st 10.5km Run; 8:45 am, Present MVP Police Award to
Brockville Police Services; 9-11:00 am, 2nd 10.5km Run; 12:00 pm, Conduct Mayor's
Challenge with Mayor Henderson at RBC – 2459 Parkedale Ave, Brockville; 1-3:00 pm
– 3rd 10.5km Run; 3-3:30 pm, Radio Interview: MyFM Gananoque; 5-7:00 pm,
4th 10.5km Run

DAY 7 Thursday, October 20th, 2016 – Ivy Lea, ON
Staying at Ambassador Hotel – 1550 Princess St, Kingston, ON
3:30 am, Wake up; 4-6:00 am, 1st 10.5km Run; 8-10:00 am, 2nd 10.5km Run; 10:00 am,
Television Interview Kingston News Corus Entertainment; 12:15 pm, Speaking at
Rotary Club of Kingston; 2-4:00 pm, 3rd 10.5km Run; 5:45 pm, Present MVP Police
Award to Lansdown OPP (Ivy Lea); 6-8:00 pm, 4th 10.5km Run

DAY 8 Friday, October 21st, 2016 – Kingston, ON
Staying at Ambassador Hotel – 1550 Princess St, Kingston, ON
Partner day with Esther & Gord Pauls (Runner's Den) – The *Run For Youth* team will
run a marathon around the City of Kingston to connect with partners.
12:00 pm, Conduct Run For Youth Mayor's Challenge with Mayor Paterson at RBC–
65 Princess Street. The Mayor's Challenge invited each city mayor to participate in the
Run For Youth by walking 1-5kms with Frederick while sharing mutual youth strategies.

DAY 9 Saturday, October 22nd, 2016 – Kingston, ON
Staying at Ambassador Hotel – 1550 Princess St, Kingston, ON
9:00 am-12:00 pm, Basketball tournament with First Nations Youth; 2:00 pm,
Speaking at Pita Pit; 2-6:00 pm, Youth concert at Sharbot Lake First Nations reserve

DAY 10 Sunday, October 23rd, 2016 – Kingston, ON
Staying at Hampton Inn – 40 McPherson Drive, Napanee, ON
3-5:00 am, 1st 10.5km Run; 7-9:00 am, 2nd 10.5km Run; 10:00 am, Speaking at Westside
Christian Reformed; 12:45 pm, Speaking at Old Navy; 1-3:00 pm, 3rd 10.5km Run; 4:30
pm, Present MVP Award to Napanee OPP; 5-7:00 pm, 4th 10.5km

DAY 11 Monday, October 24th, 2016 – Napanee, ON
Staying at Hampton Inn – 40 McPherson Drive, Napanee, ON
Media Awareness Day: Speaking/Teaching/Interviews
6:00 am, Wake up; 9-10:00 am, Speaking at Quinte Christian High School; 11:30 am,
CHML interview Bill Kelly; 12:00 pm, Speaking at Rotary Club in Belleville; 2:30
pm, Radio Interview, Napanee myFM; 3:30 pm, Speaking at RBC, 36 Dundas St. E.,
Napanee; 6-8:00 pm, Medical check-up

DAY 12 Tuesday, October 25th, 2016 – Belleville, ON
Staying at Travelodge – 11 Bay Bridge Rd, Belleville, ON
4:30am, Wake up; 5:00-7:00am, 1st 10.5km Run; 9:00-11:00am, 2nd 10.5km Run;
12:00pm, Speaking at RBC, 36 Dundas Street; 1:00-3:00pm, 3rd 10.5km Run; 3:30 pm,
Boxing at John Howard Society, 21 Wallbridge Crescent, Belleville; 4:00 pm,
Newspaper Interview: Belleville Intelligence; 4:15 pm, Radio Interview: MyFM
Belleville; 4:30-5:30 pm – Run with Quinte Christian High School, 10.5km Run

DAY 13 Wednesday, October 26th, 2016 – Belleville, ON
Staying at Travelodge – 11 Bay Bridge Rd, Belleville, ON
Partner day with Esther & Gord Pauls (Runner's Den) – The *Run For Youth* team
will run a marathon around the City of Belleville to connect with partners.
9:30-10 am, Speaking at Quinte Physio Belleville; 11-11:30 am, Speaking at RBC 241
Front Street Belleville; 1-1:30 pm, Speaking at RBC branch 366 Front Street Belleville;
2-2:30 pm, Speaking at Old Navy Quinte Mall Belleville; 4:30 pm, Present MVP Police
Award to Belleville Police Services; 6:30-7:30 pm, Speaking at Calvary Gospel Temple

DAY 14 Thursday, October 27th, 2016 – Brighton, ON
Staying at The Best Western – 930 Burnham Street, Cobourg, ON
4:30 am, Wake up; 5-7:00 am, 1st 10.5km Run; 9-11:00 am, 2nd 10.5km Run; 11:00 am,
Speaking at Beacon Youth Centre; 12:00 pm, Mayor Challenge with Brighton Mayor
Walas at RBC Brighton – 75 Main St.; 1-3:00 pm, 3rd 10.5km Run; 5-7:00 pm, 4th 10.5km
Military Run

DAY 15 Friday, October 28th, 2016 – Cobourg, ON
Staying at The Best Western – 930 Burnham Street, Cobourg, ON
4:30am, Wake up; 5:00-7:00 am, 1st 10.5km Run; 9:00-11:00 am, 2nd 10.5km Run; 11:30
am-2:00 pm, Speaking at Cobourg Rotary Club; 2:00 pm, Newspaper Interview:
Port Hope; 3-5:00 pm, 3rd 10.5km Run; 6-8:00 pm, 4th 10.5km Run

DAY 16 Saturday, October 29th, 2016 – Newcastle, ON
Staying at The Best Western – 930 Burnham Street, Cobourg, ON
4:30 am, Wake up; 5-7:00 am, 1st 10.5km Run; 9-11:00 am, 2nd 10.5km Run; 11:00 am,
Speaking at Brookside Detention Centre in Cobourg; 1-3:00 pm, 3rd 10.5km Run,
Present MVP Award to Port Hope Police Service; 5-7:00 pm, 4th 10.5km Run;
8:00 pm, Speaking at Youth Rally – Bowmanville

DAY 17 Sunday, October 30th, 2016 – Bowmanville, ON
Staying at the Comfort Inn – 533 Kingston Rd. Pickering, ON
3:30 am, Wake up; 4-6:00 am, 1st 10.5km Run; 8-10:00 am, 2nd 10.5km Run;
10:30-12:30 pm, Speaking at Liberty Pentecostal Church, Bowmanville, ON;
1:00 pm Stop at RBC, 195 King Street East, Bowmanville, Ontario/Conduct Mayor's
Challenge with Mayor Foster. Mayor Foster declared *Run For Youth* day; 1-3:30 pm,
3rd 10.5km Run; 5-7:00 pm, 4th 10.5km Run

DAY 18 Monday, October 31st, 2016 – Durham Region, ON
Staying at the Comfort Inn – 533 Kingston Rd. Pickering, ON
Media Awareness Day: Speaking/Teaching/Interviews
9:00 am, Speaking at Durham Christian High School, Bowmanville; 12:00 pm, Conduct
Mayor's Challenge with Mayor Mitchell of Whitby, ON; 2:00 pm, Oshawa Mayor
Henry – roundtable meeting to discuss youth strategies; 4:00 pm, Speaking at RBC
1050 Simcoe St. N, Oshawa

DAY 19 Tuesday, November 1st, 2016 – Pickering, ON
Staying at Chelsea Hotel Toronto – 33 Gerrard Street West, Toronto, ON
4:30 am, Wake up; 5-7:00 am, 1st 10.5km Run; 7:15 am, Speaking at Rotary Club Of
Bowmanville; 9-11:00 am, 2nd 10.5km Run; 1-3:00 pm, Start at RBC – Pickering, ON –
3rd 10.5km Run; 5-7:00 pm, 4th 10.5km Run; 6:30 pm, Speaking at Covenant House –
20 Gerrard St. E., Toronto

DAY 20 Wednesday, November 2nd, 2016 – Toronto, ON
Staying at Chelsea Hotel Toronto – 33 Gerrard Street West, Toronto, ON
Partner day run with Esther & Gord Pauls (Runner's Den) – The *Run For Youth* team
will run a marathon around the City of Toronto to connect with partners.
4:30 am, Wake up; 9:30 am, Speaking at RBC – 443 University Ave.; 10:30 am,
Speaking at RBC – 161 King St. East; 11:30 am, Speaking at RBC – 434 King St. West;
12:30 pm, Old Navy – 260 Young St.; 1:00-1:30 pm, Media Interview: Hamilton
Spectator; 2:00 pm, Speaking at John Knox Christian School, Brampton; 3:00 pm,
Speaking at Youth Detention Centre, Brampton; 6:00 pm, Present Youth Award at Mel
Lastman Square; 7:00 pm, Faith International Church – 1967 Leslie St., Toronto, ON

DAY 21 Thursday, November 3rd, 2016 – Oakville, ON
Staying at Holiday Inn, 590 Argus Rd., Oakville, ON
3:30 am, Wake up; 4-6:00 am, 1st 10.5km Run; 7:00 am, Speaking at Mississauga Rotary
Club – Patti's Diner, 2500 Meadowpine Blvd., Mississauga; 8-10:00 am, 2nd 10.5km
Run; 1-3:00 pm, 3rd 10.5km Run; 3:30 pm, RBC Cornwell – 361 Cornwall Rd in Oakville/
Present Mayor's Challenge to former Oakville Mayor Ann Mulvale; 5-7:00 pm, 4th
10.5km Run

DAY 22 Friday, November 4th, 2016 – Burlington, ON
4:30 am, Wake up; 5-7:00 am, 1st 10.5km Run; 9:00-9:30 am, Speaking at Blazing the
Agency; 10:00-10:30 am, RBC Lakeshore – 279 Lakeshore Rd. E.; 11:20 am, Media
Interview: Bill Kelly Radio Show; 1:00-3:00 pm, 3rd 10.5km Run; 4:00 pm, RBC 360 Pearl
St., Burlington, ON; Conduct Mayor's challenge with Burlington Mayor Goldring who
declared *Run For Youth* day; 4:30-6:30pm, 4th 10.5km Run; 6:30 pm, End at Liberty For
Youth Centre. Welcome Home Bonanza!

DAY 23 Saturday, November 5th, 2016 – Hamilton, ON
Road 2 Hope Marathon

RUN FOR YOUTH
WITH FREDERICK DRYDEN

WHITBY

TORONTO   PICKERING   OSHAWA

BOWMANVILLE   WELCOME   BELLEVILLE

SCARBOROUGH   COURTICE   PORT HOPE   BRIGHTON

MISSISSAUGA   NEWCASTLE   GRAFTON   DESERONTO

OAKVILLE   NEWTONVILLE   TRENTON

BURLINGTON   COBOURG   COLBORNE

HAMILTON   NAPANEE

3 WEEKS > 650km > 858,000 STEPS = $650,000 | FROM OTTAWA OCTOBER 14

JUST PICTURE IT: FREDERICK'S RUN

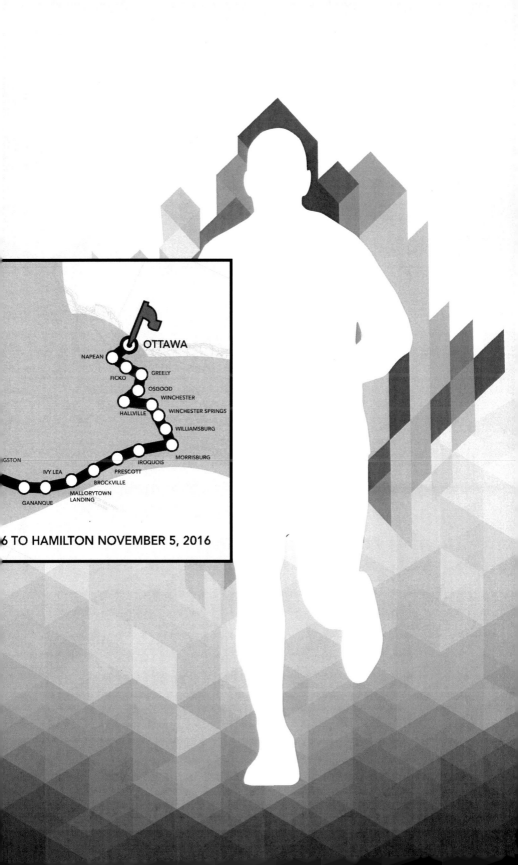

OTTAWA

NAPEAN
FICKO
GREELY
OSGOOD
WINCHESTER
HALLVILLE
WINCHESTER SPRINGS
WILLIAMSBURG
GSTON
IVY LEA
IROQUOIS
MORRISBURG
PRESCOTT
BROCKVILLE
MALLORYTOWN
GANANQUE
LANDING

6 TO HAMILTON NOVEMBER 5, 2016

Top Left: Jennifer Santamaria and Tom Palisak of RBC Royal Bank present Frederick Dryden with a $75,000 donation • Inset: Liberty For Youth's Executive Assistant, Melanie Kowalyshyn, and her mother, Julie Buck show their support • Middle left: Sharon Clark from Hamilton Port Authority presents a $50,000 cheque • Bottom: Old Navy Limeridge Mall presents their gift of $15,000

Launch (Top): Esther and Gord Pauls present a cheque for $10,000 on behalf of Runner's Den

Day 1: MP Bob Bratina and Frederick Dryden kick off the Run For Youth in Ottawa • Day 2: RBC – #909 South Keys Shopping Centre, Ottawa

Day 3: Frederick and Luis enter the town of Winchester, ON •
Day 4: The Run For Youth team completes their first of many Media
Awareness Days • Day 5: First run of the day in Johnstown, ON

Day 6: (Top photos) Mayor of Brockville, David Henderson and the Run For Youth team • (Middle left): MP Gord Brown and Frederick • (Middle right) Frederick arrives in Gananoque • (Bottom) Frederick and Luis are guests of the MyFM Gananoque radio show

Day 7: Kingston Mayor Bryan Paterson, RBC – 65 Princess Street and the Run For Youth team • Day 8: (Middle) Owner, Catherine MacLeod of Physiotherapy Kingston and Spinal Rehab Centre provides care to Frederick during his stop in Kingston • (Bottom) Frederick, Luis and Rev. Heidi De Jonge of Westside Fellowship Christian Reformed Church

Day 9: Performer Sofia and Frederick at a day-long Sharbot Lake performance • Day 10: Napanee restaurant staff welcome the Run For Youth team and provide a free dinner • Day 11: (Middle) Frederick runs with Quinte Christian High School students • (Bottom) Belleville Rotary Club show their support to the Run For Youth on their second Media Awareness Day

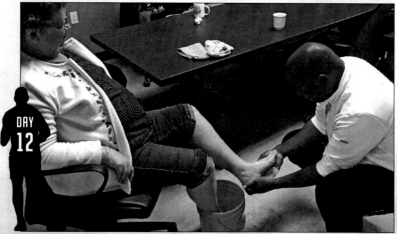

Day 11: (Top left) Napanee Inspector Pat Finnegan accepts an MVP Award on behalf of Constable Jackie Perry • (Top right) Frederick advocates for youth on Napanee myFM radio! • (Middle) RBC, 36 Dundas St. E., Napanee welcomes the Run For Youth team • Day 12: Frederick serves at the Belleville Mental Health Community Centre

Day 13: (Top) Frederick arrives in Belleville • (Middle) Family Pastor Todd Faught and the Calvary Temple Youth Group • Day 14: (Left) Old Navy in Belleville • (Right) Frederick arrives in the Hamlet of Grafton • Day 15: Cobourg Rotary Club and the Run For Youth team

Day 15: (Left) Mayor Gil Brocanier of Cobourg signs the Run For Youth map • (Middle) Northumberland-Peterborough South MP, Kim Rudd attends Cobourg's Rotary Club • Day 16: Frederick arrives in Port Hope • Day 17: Pastor Matthew Moss & Frederick at Liberty Pentecostal in Bowmanville • Day 18: (All) Bowmanville Mayor Adrian Foster declares Youth Day at RBC 195 King St. E.

Day 19: Mayor David Ryan of Pickering signs the Run For Youth map • Always friendly new faces at Old Navy • Day 20: The Run For Youth team visits Covenant House in Toronto • Bottom: RBC 443 University Avenue and the Run For Youth team

Day 20: Brampton police officers sign the Run For Youth map •
(Inset) Faith International Church with the Run For Youth team
Day 21: Frederick runs through Etobicoke being sure to get lots of
signatures as he goes

Day 22: (Top left) Former Oakville Mayor Ann Mulvale signs the Run For Youth map • (Top right) Burlington Rotarians and Frederick • (Middle) Michele & Patrick Bailey donate $10,000 to the Run For Youth • (Bottom) Home again! Frederick and his wife, Tanya, are thrilled to be reunited!

DAY
23